Collins



Revised Edition

# Vision 8

A Course on Values and Life Skills

Main menu
Learning objects
Search book or online
Page jump
Mark-up data
View fullscreen
Help menu
Bookmark page
Open tool panel
Insert note
Pen & highlight
Single/double page
Zoom in
Zoom out
Zoom 100%
Sound on/off
Record audio
Spotlight
Clear data
Interactive whiteboard mode
Collins DIGISUITE
Search here
Online Search
Page 14-15 /24
All Pages
Table of Contents
Animation
Audio
Interactivities
Teacher's Resource
Learning Tools
Test Generator
Dictionary
IWB
READING
a Read this poem and see what a sister does to take care of her little brother.
Little, helpless baby dear,
While within your cot you lie,
Sister is sitting near
She will sing your lullaby.
When at last you fall asleep,
Not the slightest noise she'll make;
Quiet as a mouse she'll keep,
Without letting her darling wake.
helpless: unable to take care of yourself
cot: a small bed with high sides for a baby
lullaby: a soft gentle song sung to make a child go to sleep
slightest: very small
quiet: making no noise
darling: a person who is loved very much by somebody
wake: to stop sleeping
26
COMPREHENSION
A. Choose the correct option.
1. The baby's sister is sitting
a. near the baby.
b. far from the baby.
c. in another room.
2. The baby's sister will
a. sing a lullaby.
b. play with the baby.
c. wake up the baby.
B. Answer the questions.
1. Where is the baby lying?
2. Who will keep quiet like a mouse?
3. How is the baby's sister? Think of and write two words to describe her.
Life Skills and Values
Caring for one's family
1. Imagine you are playing outside your house, and your little brother is sleeping inside alone. Suddenly you hear your brother cry. What would you do?
2. You are watching TV with your friend. Your sister is sleeping in the next room. Your friend asks you to raise the volume of the TV. What would you do?
27

# Preface

***Vision* Revised Edition**, a course on life skills and values, is an engaging value education series meant to enable learners lead a balanced, happy and successful life. The National Education Policy, 2020 proposes the revision and revamping of all aspects of the education structure to create a new system that is aligned with the aspirational goals of 21st century education, while building upon India's traditions and value systems. It also lays focus on critical life skills and values.

*Vision* Revised Edition follows an interactive and multidisciplinary approach and caters to all kinds of learners with different learning styles.

**Values** are presented through progressively graded stories, anecdotes or poems.

**Life Skills** as laid down by the World Health Organization (WHO) have been covered through interesting stories.

Each book contains special chapters and colourful spreads showcasing the **United Nations Sustainable Development Goals**, which are important to achieve a just and an equitable world for all.

**21st Century Skills** have been mapped to each chapter with the aim of creating well-rounded individuals thriving in a constantly changing world.

Mental health and well-being of young learners is of prime importance in today's world. Therefore, **Let's Do Yoga** poster has been introduced as a brand-new feature of the book. It contains simple and doable asanas with step-by-step guidance and illustrations.

The series also focuses on mindfulness and social-emotional learning through **'happiness activities'**. Young children learn by doing, hence the series has a variety of hands-on activities, encouraging quiet reflection and sound action.

Creating a safety net for children and making them aware of **child rights** is much needed in this age and time. *Vision* Revised Edition has special advice for children through which they can face situations in which they feel afraid, pressurized or unsafe.

*Vision* Revised Edition comes with **Collins DigiSuite** which offers digital content packed with animated stories, slideshows and interactive activities.

***Vision* Teacher's Manuals** offer comprehensive **Lesson Plans** and **Additional Worksheets** for teachers.

# In This Series ...

*Vision* Revised Edition adheres to the National Education Policy, 2020. Features such as 21st Century Skills, Life Skills, multiple intelligences, Sustainable Development Goals and Let's Do Yoga all align with the new policy.

## Discuss

Warm-up exercise familiarizes students to the mood of the chapter

## Read along

A story or a poem based on a value

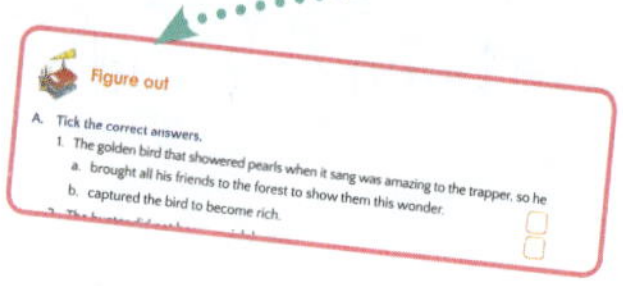


## Figure out

Questions based on the chapter to ensure value inculcation

## Relate

Application-based questions to check students' understanding

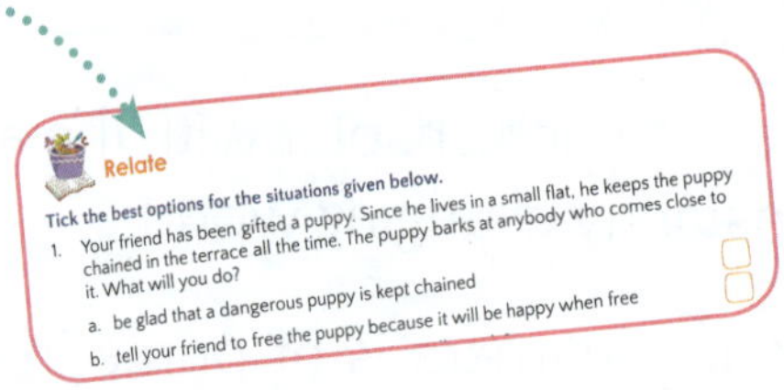


## Project

Interesting projects based on the values taught

## Happiness Activity

Interesting activities to promote 'happiness'

## Act

Interesting activities that reinforce the value taught

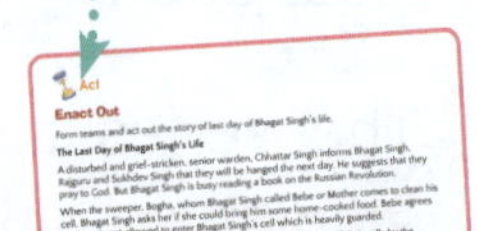


## Remember

Brief pointers that the students can incorporate in their behaviour

## Think and Say

Thinking questions that encourage students to think laterally

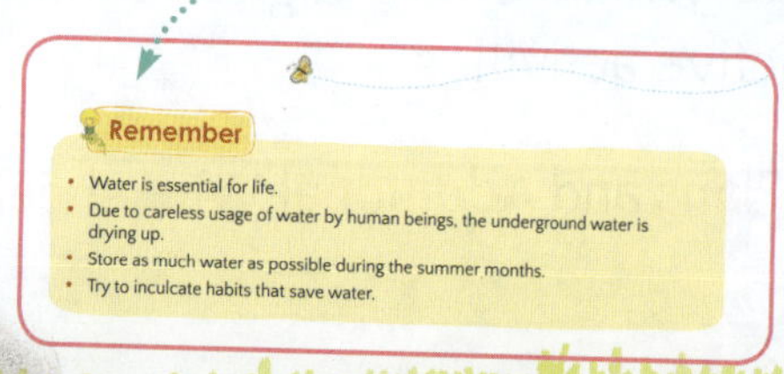


**Think and Say**

Your teacher is dictating the notes for a difficult Math topic, but your friend is absent. What will you do?

## Happiness Box

Enjoyable activities that promote 'happiness' and exercises based on multiple intelligences addressing different learning styles

- Musical
- Interpersonal
- Visual-Spatial
- Verbal linguistic
- Naturalistic
- Intrapersonal
- Logical Mathematical
- Bodily Kinesthetic

## Child Rights and Empowerment

Useful, child-centric advice to create a safety net for children and make them aware of their rights

## Sustainable Development Goals

Special chapter and a colourful spread showcasing the UN Sustainable Development Goals, a set of goals aimed at changing our world for better

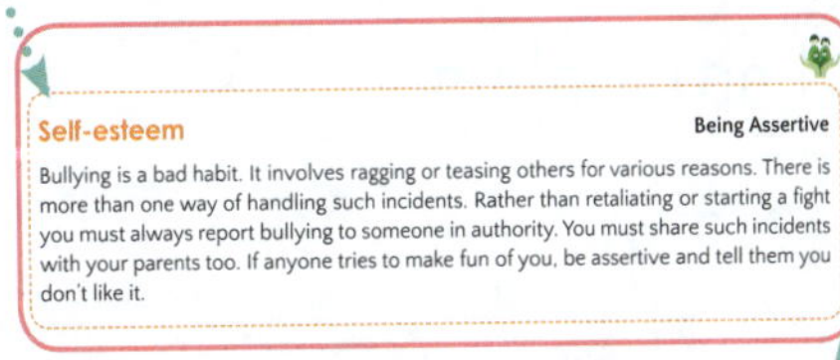

**Self-esteem** — Being Assertive

Bullying is a bad habit. It involves ragging or teasing others for various reasons. There is more than one way of handling such incidents. Rather than retaliating or starting a fight you must always report bullying to someone in authority. You must share such incidents with your parents too. If anyone tries to make fun of you, be assertive and tell them you don't like it.

## Poster

Colourful and interesting pull-out poster showcasing easy Yoga asanas

## 21st Century Skills

Skills necessary to succeed in the age of information: learning skills, literacy skills and social skills

## Life Skills

Chapters focusing on WHO life skills through interesting stories

### Teaching tips

- Emphasize that bullying must be reported and support the reportee.
- Praise students who stand up to bullying.
- Foster healthy relationships among students.

## Teaching tips

Suggestions for teachers

# Detailed Contents

## Values



## Sustainable Development Goals

## 21st Century Skills

| | | |
|---|---|---|
| Learning Skills | Communication | Be Stronger |
| Literacy Skills | Information Literacy | The Fridge that Feeds |
| | Cultural and Civic Literacy | Victory or Defeat |
| Social Skills | Tolerance and Objectivity | The Joyful Song<br>Topsy |
| | Ethical Behaviour | Don't Make Fun of Us |
| | Persistence | I am Malala |
| | Citizenship | The Incredible Dipa |
| | Flexibility | If |

## Life Skills

| | |
|---|---|
| Jakes and the Lady<br>Slotting Your Time | Empathy<br>Critical Thinking |

## Projects

| | |
|---|---|
| Project I | The Olympic Games |
| Project II | Terracotta Bath |
| Project III | Gymnastics |
| Project IV | Save Animals |

# Contents

# 1. The Joyful Song

## Discuss

**Read and discuss in class.**

'What light is to eyes; what air is to lungs; what love is to heart liberty is to the soul of man.'

## Read along

In a jungle lived a beautiful golden bird. When she sang, shining pearls fell from her open beak. A bird trapper noticed the bird and the pearls that spread around her when she sang.

He said to himself, 'Imagine how rich I will become if I own this bird'. So he spread his net and the poor golden bird was caught in it. The trapper took the bird home and kept it in a silver cage and fed it well. But the caged bird was sad, so she did not sing at all. Day after day, the hunter would come to the cage looking for the pearls. But there were none because no song came out from the throat of the sorrowful bird. When the hunter did not get any pearls, he decided to sell the bird.

The trapper sold the caged bird to a merchant. The merchant saw a beautiful golden bird and thought, 'Let me gift it to the king. He will then allow me to open a large shop in this city'.

He took the golden bird to the king. Bowing to him, he said, 'Your Majesty, please accept this gift from me'.

The king thought, 'Hmm . . . that's a nice bird. I'll give it to the princess to play with'.

### Think and Say

You see a man selling birds stuffed in a cage. The birds are pecking each other because they do not have enough place inside the cage. What will you do?

The princess was a lovely girl and she had a kind heart. She could not stand the sight of captives, whether humans, beast or bird.

She opened the silver cage at once and said, 'Come, little bird. Fly away'.

The golden bird hopped out, hardly believing it was free. The pleasure of freedom made the golden bird very happy. It joyfully opened its beak and started trilling a delightful song. As it sang loudly, pearls began to fall. One, two, three and soon a shower of pearls rained into the princess' room.

Every morning, the golden bird came to meet the princess. It sat on her window sill and sang to her.

## Remember

- Freedom is the birthright of all living creatures.
- Happiness in life is dependent on being physically, mentally and emotionally free.
- Everyone must be careful that they do not encroach on the freedom of another living creature for their own selfish needs.
- Your parents and siblings have as much right to their freedom as you do.
- While each citizen has the freedom of speech and action, we must not misuse that freedom.
- Everyone must also have the freedom of choice to select words, actions, careers and movement.

## Figure out

### A. Tick the correct answers.

1. The golden bird that showered pearls when it sang was amazing to the trapper, so he
   a. brought all his friends to the forest to show them this wonder. ☐
   b. captured the bird to become rich. ☐
2. The hunter did not become rich because
   a. the bird was too sad to sing and no pearls fell from her beak. ☐
   b. when the captured bird sang only stones fell from its beak. ☐

3. The merchant took the golden bird to the king to
   a. gift the amazing bird to the king to show his loyalty.
   b. sell the bird to the king and get in return the permission to open a big shop.
4. The princess opened the cage to free the bird because
   a. she could not bear to see animals or birds caged.
   b. she had never seen a bird fly and wanted to see if the golden bird could fly.
5. The golden bird was so happy to be free that it
   a. started singing and pearls showered from its beak.
   b. flew far away from the princess and nobody saw it again.

**B. Mahatma Gandhi said, 'Freedom is never dear at any price. It is the breath of life. Which man will not pay for living?' Do you agree with him?**

## Relate

**Tick the best options for the situations given below.**

1. Your friend has been gifted a puppy. Since he lives in a small flat, he keeps the puppy chained in the terrace all the time. The puppy barks at anybody who comes close to it. What will you do?
   a. be glad that a dangerous puppy is kept chained
   b. tell your friend to free the puppy because it will be happy when free
2. Your friend refuses to play with you. What will you do?
   a. let him have the freedom to choose whether he wants to play or study
   b. get very angry and stop talking to him
3. Your sister and you are buying ice cream and you think both should take the vanilla flavour, as that is your favourite. What will you do?
   a. force her to take a vanilla-flavoured ice cream
   b. let her choose her favourite flavour
4. Your mother is offered a job that she wants to do, but you prefer that she stays at home. What will you do?
   a. throw a tantrum about how your needs will be neglected if she takes up the job
   b. be happy for her because she deserves the freedom to choose

## Act

# Enact Out

Form teams and act out the story of last day of Bhagat Singh's life.

**The Last Day of Bhagat Singh's Life**

A disturbed and grief-stricken, senior warden, Chhattar Singh informs Bhagat Singh, Rajguru and Sukhdev Singh that they will be hanged the next day. He suggests that they pray to God. But Bhagat Singh is busy reading a book on the Russian Revolution.

When the sweeper, Bogha, whom Bhagat Singh called Bebe or Mother comes to clean his cell, Bhagat Singh asks her if she could bring him some home-cooked food. Bebe agrees but later is not allowed to enter Bhagat Singh's cell which is heavily guarded.

Next morning, Bhagat Singh, Rajguru and Suhkdev are taken out of their cells by the guards. Shouting '*Inqualab Zindabad*', they reach the jail courtyard where three officials and the hangman are waiting. The hangman gives them masks which they throw on the ground. The three freedom fighters hug each other and follow the hangman shouting 'Down with the British Empire'.

## Happiness Box

1. **After having seen the story, *The Last Day in Bhagat Singh's Life* acted out, write a play based on the story on a cartridge sheet. Make illustrations for your play on the sheet and share your illustrated plays in the class.**
2. **Read and understand this poem by Sarojini Naidu about singers who move freely wherever they wish and who believe that the world is their home.**

### Wandering Singers

Where the voice of the wind calls our wandering feet,

Through echoing forest and echoing street,

With lutes in our hands ever-singing we roam,

All men are our kindred, the world is our home.

Our lays are of cities whose lustre is shed,

The laughter and beauty of women long dead;
The sword of old battles, the crown of old kings,
And happy and simple and sorrowful things.
What hope shall we gather, what dreams shall we sow?
Where the wind calls our wandering footsteps we go.
No love bids us tarry, no joy bids us wait:
The voice of the wind is the voice of our fate.

*—Sarojini Naidu*

## Teaching tips

- Explain that there could be instances when what one considers one's freedom may make another person uncomfortable.
- Remind students that keeping any living creature in captivity is cruel.
- It is important to accept others' choices even if one may not agree with them.

# 2. Don't Make Fun of Us

## Discuss

**Read and discuss in class.**

When Mahatma Gandhi was invited to meet King George V at the Buckingham Palace in the United Kingdom, he wore only his dhoti and shawl, even though it was against the dress rules of the palace.

He announced that he had no intention of wearing any more while his countrymen remained unclothed at Britain's expense. When asked if he did not feel that he was wearing too little for his meeting with the King, Mahatma Gandhi had retorted, 'The King had enough on for both of us'.

## Read along

'The first person I called after winning the award was *Ma*, and both of us remained silent.' These humbling words were spoken by Dulal Sarkar – the man of the moment – who bagged the Best Actor Award for Kaushik Ganguly's *Chotoder Chobi*, a Bengali film, at the 45th International Film Festival of India (IFFI), Goa, on 27 March 2016. He shared the podium with another Best Actor, Alexel Serebriakov. He was awarded a Silver Peacock, certificate and cash prize.

*Chotoder Chobi*, meaning 'Little People's Picture' produced by Shree Venkatesh Films focuses on the predicaments of those born with genetic defects causing dwarfism.

However, all the applause he was receiving meant little to Sarkar, the 40-year-old 'little man' who lived in Howrah, West Bengal. He only wished to meet his mother.

When he spoke to the press, this real-life dwarf – who also plays a dwarf in the film – divulged, 'Throughout my life, I've been teased about my appearance. So, now that my work is being appreciated, I don't know how to react. I feel numb. All I want to do is touch my Ma's feet. She's my biggest support. I lost my father two years back, but I know he's up there, somewhere, blessing me.'

Dulal Sarkar regretted that people like him are not even considered physically challenged. He recalled his own pathetic experience once in a bus in Kolkata. Dulal had been sitting on the seat meant for the handicapped, but he was forced to vacate it.

**Think and Say**

You find children poking fun at a street child who crawls because his legs are bent. What will you do?

'Though I was carrying a card which said I was 60 per cent handicapped, a youth forced me to vacate the seat shouting, 'A dwarf can't be a physically challenged person', and he was supported by all other passengers. I tripped and fell on the floor in my hurry to get away from my tormenters and some of them laughed', Dulal remembered bitterly.

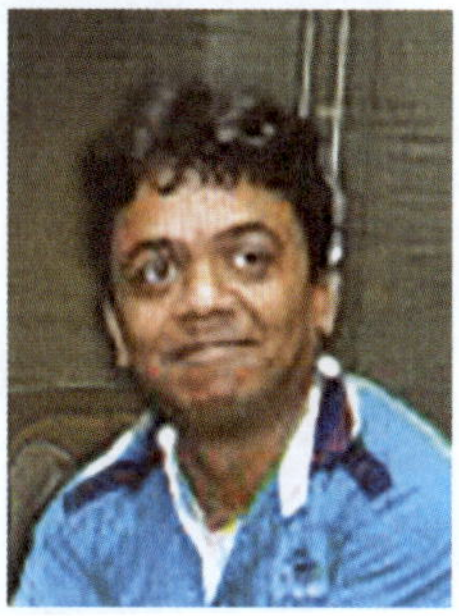

Sarkar also narrated how his classmates used to mock him. If he stood up to speak in class, everyone laughed at him. In fact, he recalled how his mother used to hide him under her sari *pallav* when she walked him to his school. She wanted to protect the child from the people on the street who pointed fingers at him as though he was a spectacle.

Presently, Dulal lives in a rented house with his mother and two brothers. 'We're five brothers, but three of them live separately with their families. I'm the only dwarf in the family. Yes, I was humiliated a lot, but I learnt to take it in my stride. I promised myself that I'll prove my worth one day', said the actor, his voice catching on the last words.

Ironically, the IFFI winner used to 'entertain' as a joker at birthday parties, marriages, the circus and melas, until recently. 'It's how I earned a living for my Ma'. As he spoke of his first reactions to winning the Award, Dulal added, 'In that silence of my first call to Ma, we were both crying. I want to buy her a nice sari from Howrah. And I'm dying to have *maach-bhaat* cooked by her'. He laughed, 'She used to love me the most, but now my nieces and nephews have taken a share of it'.

The actor admitted that he worships Kaushik Ganguly, the director of the film. 'The day I went for auditions, I could see Kaushikda had expectations from me. And since then, all I tried to do was to live up to them. He was so happy with my first shot! After all the barbs I've lived through, I was treated like an artiste for the first time on the sets of Chotoder Chobi. Kaushikda hasn't just given me a chance at life, he has given recognition to our community. 'It's my earnest request to everyone: don't make fun of us! We already have a tragic existence, trying to 'fit in' because nothing fits us,' he said.

## Remember

- No two people are the same. Some differences are just more noticeable.
- Children who are differently-abled are like all other children who want friends.
- Someone who is differently-abled deserves to be treated with same respect and dignity the same as anyone else.

- Even in a casual way, avoid using labels or offensive terms.
- Speak directly to the person, rather than to the helper standing next to him or her.
- When speaking, put yourself on the same level as the differently-abled person. Then, you can speak face to face and make the person more comfortable.
- Offer genuine help.

## Figure out

**A. Tick the correct answers.**

1. Kaushik Ganguly made the film 'Chotoder Chobi' because
   a. people find dwarfs funny and will enjoy a film about them. ☐
   b. will understand the pain and difficulties faced by dwarfs. ☐
2. Dulal Sarkar could not feel excited or happy about the Best Actor Award because
   a. he had been mocked for his appearance all his life and could not believe that he was being appreciated. ☐
   b. he had received many awards and this award was not a surprise to him. ☐
3. Sarkar's first thought on winning the award was to go to his mother because
   a. since his childhood it was his mother who had supported him. ☐
   b. his mother was an actor and wanted him to join the films. ☐
4. When he informed his mother about winning the award, she was silent because
   a. she did not believe him. ☐
   b. she was overwhelmed with emotion and was crying. ☐
5. Sarkar has great regards for the director Kaushik Ganguly because
   a. he believed that Sarkar had the potential to act in the film. ☐
   b. he is a famous film-maker ☐

**B. Elucidate the words by Dulal Sarkar, 'Kaushikda hasn't just given me a chance at life, he has given recognition to our community. It's my earnest request to everyone, don't make fun of us! We already have a tragic existence, trying to 'fit in' because nothing fits us.**

## Relate

**Tick the best options for the situations given below.**

1. You are cycling down the road and notice, at a traffic light, cars impatiently honking at a boy without feet on a small cart who uses his hands as pedals. He is not able to move fast and is holding up the queue. What will you do?
   a. just move your cycle to the free lane and go on your way ☐
   b. get off your cycle to help the child to move quickly out of the way of the cars ☐

2. Your grandfather is hard of hearing and often hears incorrect words. What will you do?
   a. help him by repeating loudly and using gestures to interpret what people say to him ☐
   b. make fun of him and feel ashamed to introduce him to your friends ☐

3. During the recess you see your visually impaired classmate about to crash into a tree. What will you do?
   a. joke about her with your friends and wait to see her fall ☐
   b. run quickly to prevent her from falling and hurting herself ☐

4. You have a cousin who is differently-abled and unable to speak clearly. He lives nearby. What will you do?
   a. spend time with him few times a week and try to play or chat with him ☐
   b. neither go to his house nor invite him home because he makes you feel uncomfortable ☐

## Act

### Find Out

Did you know that all public places are supposed to have special facilities for differently-abled people? Visit a nearby supermarket, movie hall and a hospital. Find out whether each of these places have the special facilities for people differently-abled listed in the table.

Don't forget to write down in the correct cells of the sheet the name and address of the places you go to. Display your data sheet in your class.

| | Facilities | Supermarket | Movie hall | Hospital |
|---|---|---|---|---|
| 1. | Special ramps | | | |
| 2. | Enlarged doorways for wheelchairs | | | |
| 3. | Proper listening devices and Braille signs | | | |
| 4. | Visual fire alarms | | | |
| 5. | Walks and entrances are level | | | |

## Happiness Box

**1. Make a visual heat detector which will help a differently-abled person to know that there is a fire close by.**

**Materials required**

- Rubber band
- Wood block. The wood block should be large enough for the rubber band to fit tightly around it, but not so small that it would snap the band.
- Large pin or thin nail
- Cardboard
- Scissors
- Candle and matchbox

**Method**

1. Cut the shape of an arrow from the cardboard. The arrow should be about the length of the wood block.
2. Take the rubber band and stretch it around the outer edge of your wooden block so that it's snug.
3. Push the pin through the arrow at the centre of the arrow base–the side opposite the arrow triangle.

4. Carefully place the pin under the rubber band, centred along one of the edges of the block. Take a look at the figure. Your heat detector must look like the figure.

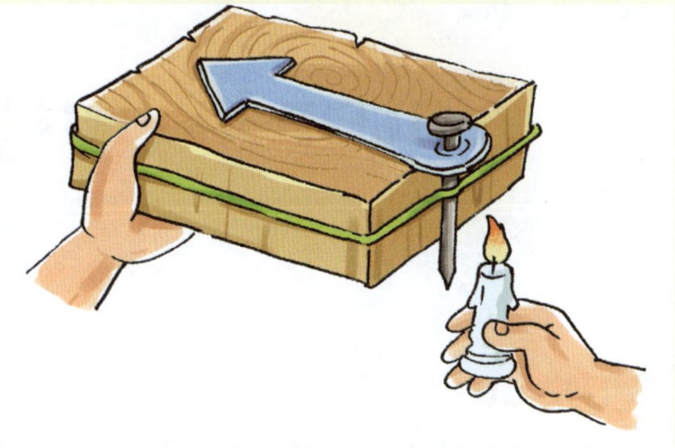

5. Light the candle and carefully bring it close to the rubber band, closest to the pin.
6. The cardboard arrow will begin to rotate anticlockwise slowly.
7. Place the candle on the opposite side of the pin.
8. The cardboard arrow will begin to rotate clockwise.

**2. Hold a brainstorming session on 'The most comfortable shopping mall for differently-abled people'. You can even hold a painting contest in your class and ask students to draw their design for a comfortable mall for differently-abled people.**

## Teaching tips

- Reiterate that children with disabilities deserve respect. They need our understanding of their situation and not pity.
- With examples of achievers such as composer Beethoven and others, explain that many people with disabilities are gifted.
- Also, explain that when a certain part of the human body is disabled, the other parts work better to make up for the disabled part. One often finds that a visually disabled person listens better than normal people and can hear sounds that others cannot.

# 3. Water Wrung Out

## Discuss

**Read and discuss in class how we consume water invisibly.**

Every human being consumes water visibly and invisibly. Visible consumption is obviously when you drink water or use it for domestic purposes. Invisible water usage or Virtual Water, a term coined by water guru, Professor Tony Allen, is the water needed to produce the goods and food we eat. This is 92 per cent of our total consumption.

## Read along

*The Sustainable Development Goal 12, Sustainable Consumption and Production, aims at 'doing more and better with less.' Sustainable consumption and production contribute significantly to poverty alleviation. This global goal is also about promoting resource and energy efficiency, sustainable infrastructure, and providing access to basic services, and a better quality of life for all.*

12 RESPONSIBLE CONSUMPTION AND PRODUCTION

**News Times**

**NO-DROUGHT VILLAGES**

SUTAPA DAS

MAY 2, 2016

Laporiya village is 85 km from Jaipur. The entire region is in the clutches of drought, yet farmers in this village are smiling. Why is that so? Even though they are on the edge of the Thar Desert where the average rainfall is just a little more than a foot, water in Laporiya's wells is at 45 feet and their crop harvest is about twelve times more than elsewhere. For twenty years, villagers of Laporiya and its nearby villages have revived ancient water conservation methods.

It is 42-year-old Laxman Singh, a feudal landlord who Laxman Singh has driven this effort. Taking a degree in social work from Rajasthan University, Singh started inciting the village community to conserve water, way back in the 80s.

Soon 98 other villages from Tonk, Jaipur and Pali joined the movement. It is now estimated that 40,000 families have benefited from this strategy applied on 30,000 hectares of land.

When the 1977 drought stuck, Singh inspired the village youth to start a campaign.

They rebuilt embankments, repaired tanks and de-silted community ponds. Then he began the *chowka* method to harvest water.

Flat pastureland on the upper levels of the village is divided into rectangular units of different sizes. Around each unit, 1.5 metre high dykes are built along the three sides that lie towards the lower slope.

Called chowkas (squares), it is a zigzag pattern that allows rainwater to enter the squares and fill them up. Excess rainwater flows into the adjoining square, and so on. So rainwater is harvested and used economically. Also these chowkas grow grass providing fodder to animals in the village. The collected outflow from the chowkas gathers in a community tank. From there it can be distributed to pastures and farmlands.

During the first years, Singh used his own money for the restoration work and labour was volunteered by the villagers. In 1986, he started a not-for-profit organization called the Gramin Vikas Navyuvak Mandal (GVNML). Through the GVNML *shramdaan* or voluntary labour became a process. It made rules to govern the holistic development of the village. The villagers together contributed money to make the dykes. Volunteers from the villages treated pastureland, rebuilt old irrigation tanks and de-silted them regularly.

The community also practised smart crop planning. They did not plant crops that needed a lot of water. During summer, only green fodder and vegetables are grown. So much fodder encouraged the villagers to keep cows that produce nearly 8-10 litres of milk. So now the villages can depend on earning from selling milk rather than only on agriculture.

Quite clearly, not just Laxman Singh's efforts, but the success of this water conservation strategy is also the result of a co-operative effort of the community. As a result, there are bumper harvests in and around Laporiya. The land that earlier yielded one crop now gives two harvests in a year.

Still, Laxman Singh knows that this kind of development can continue only by the co-operative effort of the villagers. 'Until the development process gets deeply integrated into society and the culture, the longterm success of this work may remain a big question', he says.

**Think and Say**

After recess, you are already late for class and see the drinking water taps running. What will you do?

## Remember

- Water is essential for life.
- Due to careless usage of water by human beings, the underground water is drying up.
- Store as much water as possible during the summer months.
- Try to inculcate habits that save water.

## Figure out

**A. Tick the correct answers.**

1. Despite lack of rain, the people of Laporiya are smiling because
   a. they together conserved water and can use it during the drought. ☐
   b. they are aliens who don't need water to live. ☐
2. Laxman Singh was successful in helping 40,000 families because
   a. he gave them money to buy water. ☐
   b. inspired the youth of the villages to campaign about conserving water by traditional methods. ☐
3. GVNML developed the villages by
   a. forcing the villagers to pay for the holistic development. ☐
   b. the principle of voluntary labour and donation of money for the upkeep of the dykes and tanks. ☐
4. The villagers also developed the economy of the villages by
   a. smart crop planning and diary farming. ☐
   b. inviting large corporations to start businesses. ☐
5. Continuous development is a success only when
   a. villagers are politically aware. ☐
   b. villagers volunteer their cooperative effort. ☐

**B. Explain the words, 'Droughts are result of man's insensitivity towards environment'.**

## Relate

**Tick the best options for the situations given below.**

1. You find the gardener has forgotten to disconnect the hose and the garden is flooded. What will you do?

   a. disconnect the hose and turn the tap off ☐

   b. not bother as the upkeep of the garden is not your responsibility ☐

2. You learn about water harvesting system in school. What will you do?

   a. forget about it when you reach home as school studies have no connection to real life ☐

   b. discuss with your parents if the system can be developed in your home ☐

3. Your school has decided that during summer that students of each class will spend one day in a slum to help the residents store water. What will you do?

   a. be absent the day it is your class' turn ☐

   b. eagerly fill water at the slum tube well for as many families as you can the whole day ☐

4. Coming home after playing during the summer, you love a cold shower but you know that showers use up a lot of water. What will you do?

   a. bathe with a pail and mug ☐

   b. take the shower anyway as the water used will not make much difference ☐

## Act

## Neighbourhood Survey

**Conduct a survey in your neighbourhood of 10 residents to find out the water-saving habits they practise.**

Then fill a survey data sheet with your findings and share it in the class.

**Survey data sheet**

| Nos | Water saving habits | Number of residents who do it |
|---|---|---|
| 1. | Fix leaking pipes | |

| | | |
|---|---|---|
| 2. | Ensure taps are not left flowing | |
| 3. | Avoid showers when bathing | |
| 4. | Install water harvesting systems | |
| 5. | Use waste water from kitchens to water flower pots | |

## Happiness Box

### Save Water

1. **Hold a 'World Water Day' poster contest for young children in your neighbourhood. Talk to them about ideas of how water can be saved easily and then tell them to make a poster for any one idea.**

   Put up these posters in your neighbourhood to create awareness. Also, bring the best posters to school and put them all up on a school bulletin board.

2. **Go around your school and click pictures of incidents where water is being wasted. Share your pictures during the assembly and give a short speech about saving water.**

**Teaching tips**

- Reiterate that saving water is the duty of all human beings.
- Explain when pouring water in a glass to drink, one should only pour as much as one wants.
- Remind students to fi nd out ways of using water drained from the kitchen or washing machines.

# 4. Be Stronger



## Discuss

Read the following and discuss in class.

*Bullies are:*

*NOT COOL*

*NOT FRIENDLY*

*NOT POPULAR*

*NOT RESPECTED*

*NOT WELCOME*

*√ ALL OF THE ABOVE*

## Read along

I'm sure you don't remember who I am,
But I haven't forgotten a single thing.
You may now know me as a fighter,
But I used to be a victim of bullying.

For every time you broke my glasses,
I fill my desk with flower vases.
For every day you made me cry,
I help a stranger to get by.
For all the pain you made me feel,
I make another dream become real

I was the kid that hid in corners
Because you pushed and shoved me around.
I was the quiet shadow in the back
Because your cruelty silenced my every sound.
I was always the lonely odd one out
Because you filled me with doubt.

But now I'm stronger;
I don't cower any longer.
But now I'm wiser;
Can be calm without a tranquilizer.
But now I'm unashamedly me;
Proud of myself for all to see.

For every time you broke my mug,
I comfort someone with a hug.
For every day you pulled my hair,
I teach someone how to be fair
For all the times you cut me off ,
I show someone the path to love.

I'm sure you don't remember me
Because I was just dirt crushed under your boots.
But let me tell you I'm now free
And work as a teacher to eliminate bullying by its roots.

*—Devika Fernando*

## Self-esteem

**Being Assertive**

Bullying is a bad habit. It involves ragging or teasing others for various reasons. There is more than one way of handling such incidents. Rather than retaliating or starting a fight you must always report bullying to someone in authority. You must share such incidents with your parents too. If anyone tries to make fun of you, be assertive and tell them you don't like it.

## Remember

- Lend support if you find students younger or weaker than you being bullied.
- Always report bullying because you will help others too.
- If you find somebody bullying, instantly prevent it.
- Become part of group activities
- Support a student being bullied by praising their strong qualities.
- Be an example to the younger students and your peers.
- Never ignore any complaints that may sound like bullying.

## Figure out

**A. Tick the correct answers.**

1. The man does not recognize the poet whom he used to bully when both were students because
   a. the poet is now known as a person who fights injustice. ☐
   b. the poet has now grown into a big and tall man himself. ☐
2. When the poet was a boy, he always hid himself because
   a. he was scared of the darkness. ☐
   b. he was scared of being pushed and shoved around by the bully. ☐
3. The poet became sick and had to take medicines because
   a. of some infection that he had caught in the school. ☐
   b. of his constant fear of being bullied in school. ☐
4. When he grew up, he decided to get rid of his hatred of bullies by
   a. hiring bodyguards to protect him. ☐
   b. helping strangers, teaching others to be fair and showing somebody how to love. ☐
5. Though the bully does not remember him, the poet decides to be remembered
   a. for the way he punished his tormentor in school. ☐
   b. for his efforts to remove bullying from schools forever. ☐

**B. 'People who pull you down are actually much weaker than you are'. Do you agree?**

## Relate

**Tick the best options for the situation give below.**

1. You see a big dog growling at a small puppy because it wants the puppy's bone. What will you do?
   a. chase the bigger dog away and make sure it does not come back ☐
   b. walk away thinking it is not your problem ☐
2. A driver of an expensive car is shouting at a rickshaw puller who came close to his car though it is the car that is in the wrong lane. What will you do?
   a. tell your father to drive past because you don't want to be involved in a street fight ☐
   b. request your father to stop and stand up against the injustice to the rickshaw puller ☐
3. You come to know that a gang of rowdy boys has broken the flower pots of the elderly lady who is your neighbour. What will you do?
   a. just take a look at the broken flower pots and go off to play ☐
   b. buy some flower pots with your pocket money and help her replant them and then get a complaint written against the boys at the society office ☐
4. A small and thin classmate wants to join your basketball team but the stronger team members push and shove him off the court. What will you do?
   a. stand and watch the incident because you are part of the team ☐
   b. stand up against the team members and make special efforts to ensure that your weaker classmate not only plays but is not bullied by the others ☐

## Act

# Anti-bullying Week

### Have an Anti-bullying Week

It is a week-long event which encourages everyone to take an active role to prevent bullying in the school. The focus is on both personal and community responsibilities to address the problem of bullying through media campaigns, classroom activities and workshops.

Here are some activities your class can coordinate.

1. Put up in all classes, in the corridors and in the playground a sign that looks like this.
2. You can request some of your teachers to conduct workshops for students on 'How to Deal with Bullying'.
3. Your class makes teams of four students each who hold discussion sessions in junior classes to explain what is bullying and the reasons for it.

Some discussion points:

- What does the word 'bully' make you think of?
- Where can bullying happen?
- Why would one child want to bully another?

## Happiness Box

1. **Have an art event as part of your Anti-Bullying Week.**
2. **Read and understand this poem by Sarojini Naidu about singers who move freely wherever they wish and who believe that the world is their home.**

   Make three groups in your class. Each group can pick one topic from the following and make a picture illustrating it.

   1. How does a bully feel?
   2. How does a victim feel?
   3. How does a bystander feel?

   Share the artwork on a school bulletin board and let students comment on them.
3. **Choose a student from a junior class as your pupil. You will teach your pupil to identify bullying actions and give him or her the strength to have zero tolerance towards it.**

   You can make this pamphlet and share with your pupil.

**Stop bullying**

**Zero tolerance to all forms of bullying**

We will stand up against

**Stop bullying**

### Physical bullying

- Hitting, kicking, or pushing someone or even just threatening to do it.
- Stealing, hiding or destroying someone's things.
- Making someone do things he or she does not want to do.

**Stop bullying**

### Verbal bullying

- Name-calling
- Teasing
- Insulting

**Stop bullying**

### Relationship bullying

- Refusing to talk to someone.
- Spreading lies or rumours about someone.
- Making someone do things he or she doesn't want to do.

### Teaching tips

- Emphasize that bullying must be reported and support the reportee.
- Praise students who stand up to bullying.
- Foster healthy relationships among students.
- Take all complaints of bullying seriously.

# 5. I am Malala

## Discuss

**Read Malala Yousafzai's statement and discuss in class.**

## Read along

Malala was in her class when she was informed that she had been awarded the 2014 Nobel Prize for Peace and she would share it with Mr Kailash Satyarthi, an Indian Child Rights activist. For Malala, this was an unexpected honour. She was thrilled thinking how proud her parents will be.

Her thoughts went back to when it had all started. 9 October 2012 was a bright, sunny afternoon when she boarded her school bus. Sitting between two of her friends, Malala had been thinking about revising the lesson taught the day before. Suddenly, the girls heard the brakes screech and the bus had halted. All of them leaned out to see. Malala felt

a hand on her shoulder. When she turned, a pair of cold and empty eyes bore into hers. The silence around her was deafening. Malala saw the man's lips move, but couldn't hear anything. Her face felt numb. Then, she heard the man's words. He was asking, who was Malala . . .

None of the girls spoke but some looked at her.

His other hand came up. There was a gun in it. He pointed it at Malala. In that moment of shock and horror, she understood what this was all about. The echo of the gunshot filled the air as he had fired...but she could only close her eyes and think of her parents.... How she wished her father and family were with her so that she could see them for one last time. Malala remembered thinking how could she die...so soon, without doing all that she had wanted to do? Who would fight for her sisters?

With these thoughts in her mind, she had felt the bullet tear into her flesh. The pain was terrible...and then a chill stole over Malala. She fell into a blackness...

She came to know much later that two of her friends had also been shot, one in the hand and the other in the shoulder. Only Malala had been seriously injured. The bullet went through her left eye socket, out of the back of the head and into her shoulder. Thankfully, she had sunk into a soft woolly darkness. There were times when she had come out of it but it was too painful and she had relapsed into the darkness. Her father had told her, later, that it was the Pakistan Army doctors who had treated her first. They had operated on her head. But soon, her other organs started failing. By then, the entire world had begun condemning the attack. Even Mr Ban Ki-moon, the UN Secretary General had called it, 'a heinous crime . . .'. Many offers hadstarted coming from America, Germany and UK to treat Malala free in their best hospitals. Eventually, she had been shifted to the Queen Elizabeth hospital at Birmingham, in UK.

A week after being shot, when Malala opened her eyes, she was in a strange green room. It was the ICU of Queen Elizabeth Hospital. Her parents could not accompany her as their passports and visas were still being arranged. Malala had been a bit nervous, especially as she could not speak English very well. But the doctors had been very compassionate and a Muslim lady cleric spoke to Malala in Urdu. She had been told the bullet had not touched her brain. Malala had given silent thanks to God. Wasn't it due to Allah's grace that she had been given another chance to fulfil her mission?

As she became stronger, Malala was convinced that she had been reborn . . . reborn for a reason. Allah had given her another chance—a chance to do her work. She still did not understand why she had been gifted a bullet through her head for fighting for a girl child's basic rights . . . Her only 'crime' had been to fight for female education. Malala had lived in the Swat Valley in Khyber Pakhtunkhwa province of Northwestern Pakistan. She had defied the local law. Not only had she gone to school herself, but she had helped other girls there to attend school. Her parents had always fully supported her in her beliefs.

Malala believes that everything happens for a reason. This attack has brought Malala international attention and support and made her fight that much stronger. The best outcome has been the ratification of Pakistan's First Right to Education Bill. Mr Gordon Brown, UN Special Envoy for Global Education launched a petition demanding all children worldwide be in school by the end of 2015. Its slogan 'I am Malala' has become globally famous. She has also been nominated for the International Children's Peace Prize by the South African activist, Desmond Tutu. Malala was overwhelmed when she was invited officially to open the Library of Birmingham! What an honour!

The loud sound of clapping by her classmates and teachers zipped Malala back to the present. They were congratulating her for the Nobel Prize.

Malala Yousafzai was just 17 years old in 2014, the youngest Nobel Prize recipient! She is proud not only for herself but for all young girls around the world . . . And she also feels afraid! This worldwide recognition and awards mean the responsibility of completing her mission lies even more heavily on her young shoulders. She is waiting for her dream to become a reality, which will be when she is welcomed back into her country.

Meanwhile, Malala cannot forget even for a moment that she has been given a second chance at life!

The Nobel Committee statement, accompanying her Award, says, 'Despite her youth, Malala Yousafzai has already fought for several years for the right of girls to

**Think and Say**

You see a little boy running after a ball right into the traffic-filled road. What will you do?

education and has shown by example that children and young people, too can contribute to improving their situations'.

## Remember

- Courage is that which makes you stand up and speak.
- Fighting all kinds of injustice needs courage.
- Courage is not the absence of fear. It is overcoming fear.
- It needs courage to go on when you don't have strength.
- When we say, 'I will try again tomorrow', we are courageous.
- Courage is never giving up.

## Figure out

**A. Tick the correct answers.**

1. Why could Malala not hear at first what the man was saying?
   a. There was too much noise in the bus. ☐
   b. She was stunned because she could sense danger from the man. ☐
2. When she knew she was going to die, what were her thoughts?
   a. She wanted to see her father and family and she regretted that her work was incomplete. ☐
   b. She was frightened and wanted to ask for mercy. ☐
3. Why did the UN Secretary General call the attack on Malala, 'a heinous crime'?
   a. Malala was just a child who had tried to take the girls of her region to school. ☐
   b. Malala was a child whom the terrorists had forced to attack schools. ☐
4. Why was Malala attacked?
   a. She was telling all the people in the Swat region to fight the militants. ☐
   b. She was working for female education in the Swat region. ☐
5. Why did Malala feel afraid when she was given awards and honours?
   a. She was afraid that they will be stolen from her. ☐
   b. She felt even more responsible to complete her task of bringing education to all the girls of Pakistan. ☐

**B.** **Explain what you understand by the words, '. . . has shown by example that children and young people, too can contribute to improving their own situations.'**

## Relate

**Tick the best options for the situations given below.**

1. You are passing a house, and through the window, you see a young man intimidating an old woman. What will you do?
   a. run away because if the man sees you, he may harm you ☐
   b. quickly call an adult or a police officer to help the old woman ☐
2. You are cycling on the road and you see a man push a girl, snatch her bag and run. What will you do?
   a. instantly chase him on your cycle and shout loudly to the people around to catch the thief ☐
   b. ignore the incident and try to move away from the area quickly ☐
3. You are clicking photographs at a zoo and you hear two men discussing about kidnapping a small child. What will yo do?
   a. move away as fast as possible as they might attack you? ☐
   b. try to click their photos and show it to the zoo guards so that they can be caught? ☐
4. A little child is being attacked by a ferocious dog in a park. What will yo do?
   a. throw stones or shout at the dog to divert it, so that the child can escape
   b. avoid the dog and the child and hurriedly move away from the situation

## Act

# Celebrating Failures

**Why should we be afraid of failing? Let us celebrate failures.**

Each student will come up to the front of the class and tell an imaginary story of what he or she failed at that day. Once the student completes the story, the rest of the class will applaud him or her. The student must also bow deeply to accept the celebration of his or her failure.

Some imaginary failure stories could be:

- I put my blue jeans in the washing machine with the other clothes and now all the clothes are blue.
- I forgot to close the garden gate and now all the flowers have been chewed off by the cows that entered the garden.
- After playing, I took off my shoes and left them on the lawn all night. It rained and now my shoes are soaking wet.

## Happiness Box

1. **Make a Wall of Courage on your class display board.**

   Each student must write out briefly a true story of a courageous person along with a photo or a printout of his her picture. Stick the stories on the wall throughout the week. On the next Monday, invite the other classes to view your class' 'Wall of Courage' during the recess.

2. **Create an advertisement with the heading, 'Looking for a Superhero'. Write down all the qualities the person must have and details of the job that the superhero will do. Make your advertisement interesting and attractive.**

### Teaching tips

- Explain that courage is not always momentary; bearing difficulties for a long period of time also needs courage.
- Remind students that really brave people are found in life, not in stories or films.
- Tell students to read the stories of the children who win the President's Bravery Award every year.

# 6. Topsy

## Discuss

**Look at the picture and discuss in class whether the village children have the right attitude.**

## Read along

*Uncle Tom's Cabin, written in 1852, is about African American slaves such as Uncle Tom, Topsy and other slaves. The story shows the cruelty of slavery and is regarded as one of the major causes of the American Civil War.*

Topsy was one of the blackest of her race; and her round shining eyes, glittering as glass beads, moved with quick and restless glances over everything in the room. Her mouth, half-open with astonishment at the wonders of the new master's parlour, displayed a white and brilliant set. Her woolly hair was braided in sundry little tails, which stuck out in every direction. The expression on her face was an odd mixture of shrewdness and cunning, over which was oddly drawn, like a veil, an expression of the most doleful gravity and solemnity. She was dressed in a single, filthy, ragged garment, made of bagging and stood with her hands demurely folded before her. Altogether, there was something odd and goblin-like about her appearance.

Miss Ophelia said to St. Clare, 'Augustine, why in the world have you brought that thing here for?'

'For you to educate, to be sure, and train in the way she should go.'

Miss Ophelia saw that there was nobody that would undertake to oversee the cleansing and dressing of the new arrival, so she was forced to do it herself, with some very ungracious and reluctant assistance from Jane.

Then sitting down before her, Miss Ophelia began to question her.

'How old are you, Topsy?'

'Dunno, Missis,' said the image, with a grin that showed all her teeth.

'Don't know how old you are? Didn't anybody ever tell you? Who was your mother?'

'Never had one!' said the child, with another grin.

'Never had any mother? What do you mean? Where were you born?'

'Never was born!' persisted Topsy, with another grin, that looked so goblin-like.

'Have you ever heard anything about God, Topsy?'

The child looked bewildered, but grinned as usual.

'Do you know who made you?'

'Nobody, as I knows on,' said the child, with a short laugh.

Miss Ophelia thought she would turn her inquiries to something more tangible.

'What can you do?'

'Fetch water, and wash dishes, and rub knives, and wait on folks.'

Miss Ophelia rose from this encouraging colloquy; St. Clare was leaning over the back of her chair.

'You find virgin soil there, Cousin; put in your own ideas,—you won't find many to pull up.'

Miss Ophelia began with Topsy by taking her into her chamber, the first morning, and solemnly commencing a course of instruction in the art and mystery of bed-making.

A fluttering fragment of the ribbon hanging out of one of her sleeves caught Miss Ophelia's attention. Instantly, she pounced upon it. 'What's this? You naughty, wicked child, you've been stealing this!'

The ribbon was pulled out of Topsy's own sleeve, yet was she not in the least disconcerted; she only looked at it with an air of the most surprised and unconscious innocence.

'Laws! why, that ar's Miss Feely's ribbon, an't it? How could it a got caught in my sleeve?

'Topsy, you naughty girl, don't you tell me a lie—you stole that ribbon!'

'Missis, I declar for 't, I didn't.'

'Now, Topsy," said Miss Ophelia, 'confess all about it.'

'Laws, Missis! I took Miss Eva's red thing she wears on her neck.'

'You did, you naughty child! Well, what else?'

'I took Rosa's yer-rings—them red ones.'

Just at this moment, Eva came innocently into the room, with the identical coral necklace on her neck.

'Why, Eva, where did you get your necklace?' said Miss Ophelia.

'Get it? Why, I've had it on all day,' said Eva.

Miss Ophelia looked perfectly bewildered; the more so, as Rosa, at that instant, came into the room, with a basket of newly-ironed linen poised on her head, and the coral ear-drops shaking in her ears!

'I'm sure I can't tell what to do with such a child!' she said, in despair. 'What in the world did you tell me you took those things for, Topsy?'

'Why, Missis said I must 'fess; and I couldn't think of nothin' else to 'fess,' said Topsy, rubbing her eyes.

Eva stood looking at Topsy.

Tere stood the two children, representatives of the two extremes of society. The fair, highbred child, with her golden head, her deep eyes, her spiritual, noble brow, and prince-like movements; and her black, keen, subtle, cringing, yet acute neighbour . . .

Something, perhaps, of such thoughts struggled through Eva's mind. But a child's thoughts are rather dim, undefined instincts; and in Eva's noble nature many such were yearning and working, for which she had no power of utterance. When Miss Ophelia expatiated on Topsy's naughty, wicked conduct, the child looked perplexed and sorrowful, but said, sweetly, 'Poor Topsy, why need you steal? You're going to be taken good care of now. I'm sure I'd rather give you anything of mine, than have you steal it.'

It was the first word of kindness the child had ever heard in her life, and the sweet tone and manner struck strangely on the wild, rude heart, and a sparkle of something like a tear shone in the keen, round, glittering eye, but it was followed by the short laugh and habitual grin.

**Think and Say**

It is your birthday and you are carrying a bag of sweets for friends at school. When your bus stops at a red light, you give a sweet to a street child. Soon, all the street children close by, come running for sweets. What will you do?

St. Clare, Eva's father, took amusement in the child. Topsy, whenever her sins brought her into disgrace in other quarters, always took refuge behind his chair, and St. Clare, in one way or other, would make peace for her.

From him, she got many a stray picayune, which she laid out in nuts and candies, and distributed, with careless generosity, to all the children in the family; for Topsy, to do her justice, was a good-natured and liberal child.

— *Extracted and adapted from Uncle Tom's Cabin by Harriet Beecher Stowe.*

## Remember

- Be supportive to people who are in any kind of discomfort.
- Everyone has adjustment problems to new situations.
- Patiently deal with people who may take time to grasp ideas.
- Avoid labelling people according to your own observations.
- Avoid judging people. There is always a reason for an action.
- Be friendly and free from prejudices.

## Figure out

**A. Tick the correct answers.**

1. Why did St. Clare bring Topsy to his sister, Miss Ophelia?
   a. He wanted his sister to educate and train Topsy. ☐
   b. He wanted his sister to use Topsy as a servant. ☐
2. What do you guess when Topsy said that she had never been born?
   a. Topsy is not a human being. ☐
   b. Topsy must have been taken from her mother as a baby, so she does not recall any family who would tell her how she had been born. ☐
3. Why did Topsy lie that she had stolen things?
   a. Topsy was eager to obey Miss Ophelia and had not been taught that lying was wrong. ☐
   b. Topsy lied because she enjoyed it. ☐

4. What do you think were the thoughts in Eva's mind when she looked at Topsy?
   a. Eva thought Topsy was a lesser human being than she was.
   b. Eva realized that Topsy needed all the support, kindness and love that Eva could give her.
5. Why did Topsy share the nuts and candies that St. Clare gave her with the other children?
   a. Despite being uneducated, selfishness was not in Topsy's nature so she instinctively shared things.
   b. Topsy wanted to show off to the other children how much St. Clare loved her.
6. What did Eva say when Miss Ophelia asked her about the necklace?
   a. 'Why I have had it on all day'
   b. 'I got it from Topsy'

**B. Explain the words: '. . . the sweet tone and manner struck strangely on the wild, rude heart, and a sparkle of something like a tear shone in the keen, round, glittering eye.'**

## Relate

**Tick the best options for the situations given below.**

1. You are surprised to recognize the new student in your class as the son of your driver. What will you do?
   a. refuse to acknowledge that you know him
   b. greet him in a friendly manner and offer all help
2. Your friend has decided to leave the school as it admits children from economically weaker sections of the society and he does not want to study with them. What will you do?
   a. try to convince him that respect is dependant not on birth but on merit
   b. agree with him and request your parents to change your school
3. Your house help wears a strong-smelling hair oil which makes you feel sick. What will you do?
   a. tell your mother that she must get some other house help
   b. politely request your house help if she can wear a hair oil that is mildly scented

4. A cricket team consisting of boys from the slum want to play a match with your team at the park. What will you do?
   a. welcome the team as your opponent team and arrange the match ☐
   b. snub the team and scold them for daring to suggest such a thing ☐
5. One of your friends likes to wear colourful bright clothes. What will you do?
   a. Laugh and poke fun at him ☐
   b. Appreciate his choice of clothes ☐

## Act

## Let's Interview

**Interview at least one student who has been admitted through the Economically Weaker Section quota. You can ask the following questions.**

1. Coming here from your previous school, what were the difficulties of adjustment that you faced?
2. In what ways will your studying in this school benefit you?
3. How do your classmates support you?
4. How do you support your classmates?
5. After knowing about your experience, have friends from your previous school wanted to move to our school?
6. What does your family feel about your change of school?

## Happiness Box

**1. Gifts for Friends**

1. Labelling people can be helpful but it can also be misleading.
2. Make groups of five students each. Imagine your group has gone on a holiday to London. Get a gift for any five of your classmates.
3. First write down the names of the five classmates your group has selected to give a gift. Next to each name write their interests or hobbies. Then, write down your group's choice of a gift for each.
4. Each group reads out the gifts chosen for the five classmates and asks them if these were good choices.

| No. | Names | Interests | Gifts |
|---|---|---|---|
| 1. | Amrita | Dancing | |
| 2. | Sahil | Indoor games | |
| 3. | Deepa | Cooking | |
| 4. | Kiran | Reading | |
| 5. | Barun | Cricket | |

**2. Your school runs a *'Shiksha Kendra'* for the weaker sections of the society. You volunteer to teach these underprivileged children after the school hours. It has been a fulfilling experience for you. Write about it in your diary.**

## Teaching tips

- Emphasize that empathy offered when somebody is in distress will be returned when you need support.
- Reiterate that all new students need help which should be given unequivocally.
- Encourage peer relationships that foster respect.

# Happiness Activity

**During times of emergency, our safety is our happiness. Read the precautions you should take during the COVID-19 pandemic.**

Wash your hands often

Use alcohol-based hand sanitizer

Wear a surgical mask if you are sick

Cover coughs and sneezes

Use shirt arm while coughing if you don't have tissue paper

Avoid close contact with people who are sick

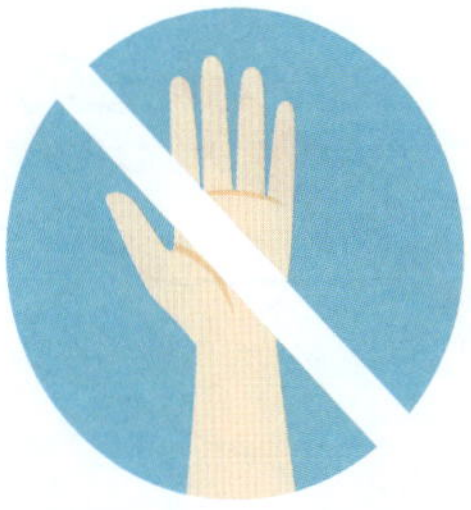
Avoid touching your eyes, nose or mouth with unwashed hands

Stay home if you're sick

Avoid crowds

Clean and disinfect

Discard used tissue paper

When a natural disaster occurs, we can't always rely on police or governments to provide help. It is always better to have one's own disaster kit. Look at the pictures and tick the things you will keep in your disaster kit.

1

2

3

4

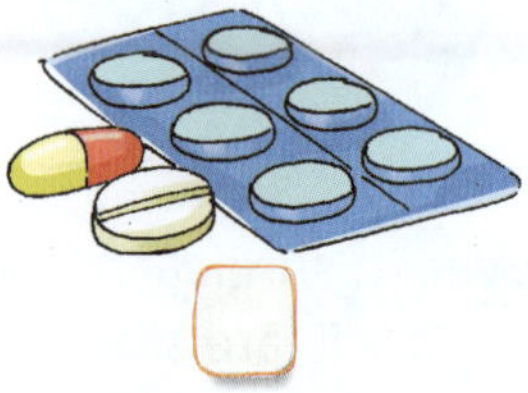

5

6

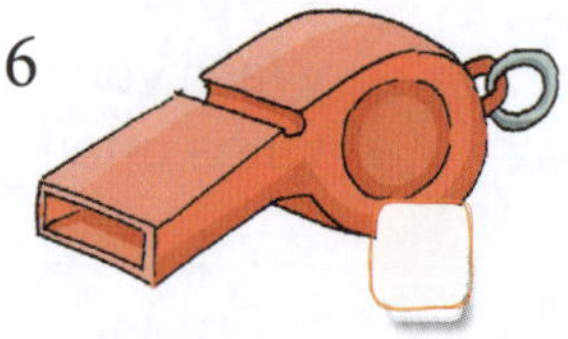

7

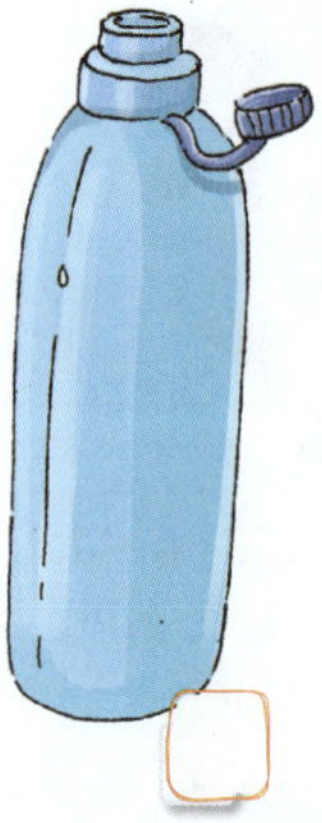

8

9

10

11

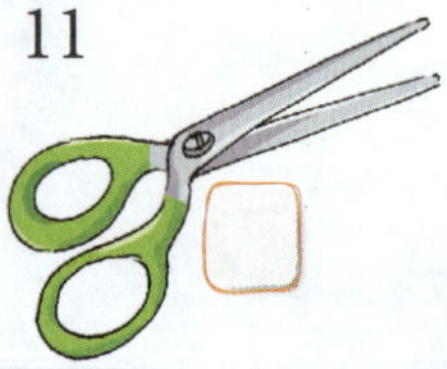

12

13

14

15

16

17

18

19

20

21

22

23

24

26

25

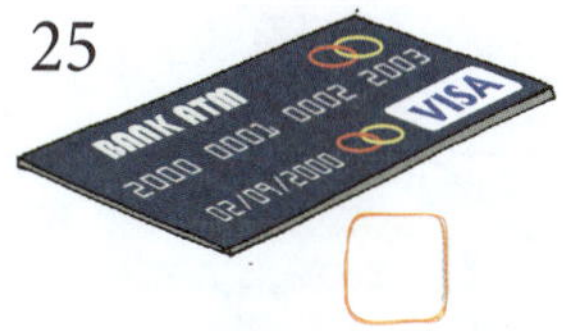


27

**Use the clues to write the words related to safety during pandemic.**

1. Maintaining as little contact as possible in public places. (2 words, 16 letters)

   ..........................................................................................

2. A mouth and nose covering that can protect us from contracting the coronavirus. (4 letters)

   ..........................................................................................

3. Staying home during the pandemic. (10 letters)

   ..........................................................................................

4. Short form of a protective gear worn by healthcare workers to stay safe. (3 letters)

   ..........................................................................................

5. A liquid disinfectant we should carry wherever we go during the pandemic. (9 letters)

   ..........................................................................................

6. A very important precaution to avoid falling sick during the pandemic. (2 words, 11 letters)

   ..........................................................................................

7. We must avoid this as much as possible during the pandemic. (6 letters)

   ..........................................................................................

8. A transparent protective covering for the face. (2 words, 10 letters)

   ..........................................................................................

## *Social Distancing*

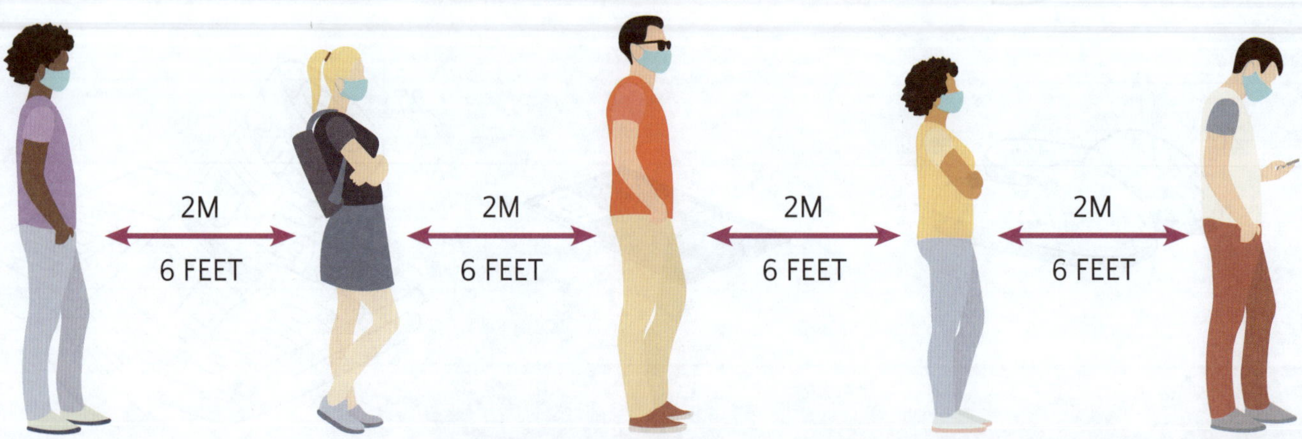

# Project I : The Olympic Games

**Let's gather information about the Olympic Games. Make groups of five students each.**

**Each student will take the responsibility of the following five areas of the topic. Collect data such as interesting information, pictures and historical data about each area.**

1. The Ancient Olympic Games
2. The Olympic Flame
3. The Olympic Rings
4. The Olympic Pledge
5. The True Spirit of Sportsmanship medal

Put together all the information to design a presentation.

Each group will use a PowerPoint presentation, pictures and role play to present the information collected to the class.

# Project II : Terracotta Birdbath

**Create your own birdbath with terracotta pots and saucer.**

**Materials required**

- Terracotta flower pots
- Clay saucer
- Paints in assorted colours suitable for your design.
- Water-based sealant for sealing the painted surfaces of your project
- Oil-based acrylic paint for sealing the insides of the flower pots
- Paint brushes, sponges, stencils and stamps
- Liquid Construction Adhesive

**Method**

1. Rub away any sand, rough spots or loose clay particles on the rim, bottom edge, and outside of the pots and saucer.
2. Stack the pots, starting with the largest pot, upside down, on the bottom, then the medium-sized pot, then the smallest pot on top.
3. Fill soil in the bottom and sow the seeds. Water the soil lightly.

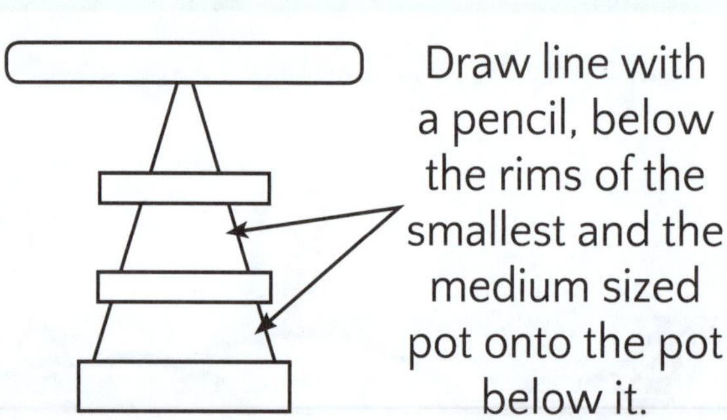


4. Draw a line with a pencil, below the rims of the small and medium-sized pot onto the pot below it. This will help you know the area that will be exposed when the pots are stacked. You can draw designs on the exposed parts only.
5. Seal the inside of all the pots and the saucer with three coats of oil-based acrylic paint. Also seal the lower edge of the largest pot, that is, the edge that will rest on the ground.
6. Now that the pots and the saucer are sealed inside and dry, they can be painted with your choice of base paint. You can make each pot a with different color, or they can all be the same.

7. When you have finished decorating or painting your birdbath, let it dry thoroughly.
8. Then seal the entire outside, even the unpainted outside areas of the pots, with at least three coats of water-based sealant.

### Install your birdbath

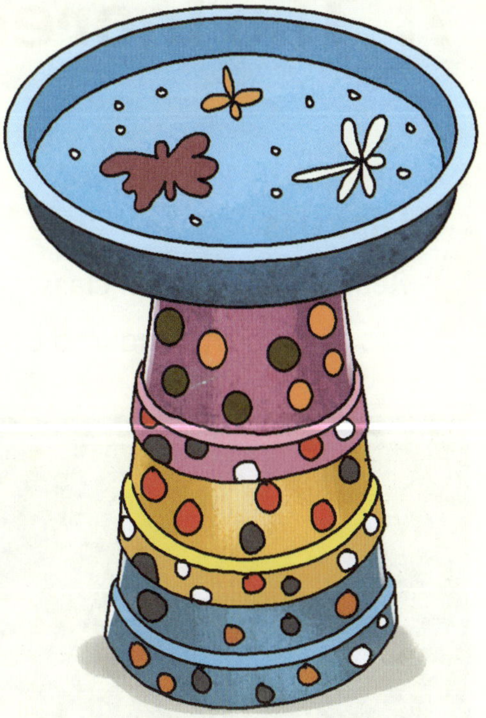

- Glue the saucer to the smallest pot. Run a generous amount of liquid adhesive on the smallest pot where it will be attached to the saucer.
- Turn the saucer over on the floor and place the small pot in the center of saucer bottom.
- Let it dry overnight.
- Now stack the pots as you had done it earlier with the clay saucer on top.
- Fill water in the saucer and enjoy watching the birds play and bathe in your birdbath.

# 7. The Incredible Dipa

## Discuss

**Read and discuss in class.**

'It's always an honour to be able to represent your country at the highest level'

## Read along

Dipa Karmakar was the first Indian gymnast to qualify for the Olympics after 52 years.

She is the only female gymnast from India to participate in the Olympics. She had been selected for the women's Artistic Gymnastics event for 2016 Summer Olympics. Born on 9 August 1993, Karmakar hails from Agartala, Tripura and started practising gymnastics when she was 6 years old. She has been coached by veteran Bisbeshwar Nandi who remains her coach even now. Nandi recalled, 'I still remember Dipa coming to me as a flatfooted kid. This physical impediment is not good for a gymnast. It affects the spring in her jump'. He added, 'That was the hardest part to fix for Dipa. We had to work very, very hard when she was a little kid to get the curve in her feet'.

Dipa's father was a coach with the Sports Authority of India. Despite her foot problem, he wanted her to try for gymnastics. So he introduced her to it even though Dipa was reluctant. In 2007, when she won at the Junior Nationals in Jalpaiguri, she became keen to excel at the sport. She was part of the 2010 Indian gymnastics contingent at the Delhi Commonwealth Games. The next year, Karmakar won five gold medals in floor, vault, all around, balance beam and uneven bars at the 2011 National Games of India, representing Tripura.

Dipa got the spotlight last year at the Commonwealth Games held in Glasgow, Scotland and won a bronze medal, making it India's first-ever medal by a woman gymnast in the CWG.

Consequently, Dipa Karmakar, on 18 April 2016 created history by becoming the first Indian woman gymnast to qualify for Olympics as she booked a berth for the Rio Games after a strong performance. Consequently, she qualified for the final vault event at the 2016 Olympics that took place on 10 August.

Apart from being the first Indian woman, she also became first from the country to qualify for the quadrennial extravaganza. Her final score, along with the difficult Produnova, gave Dipa 15.066 points, and she finished with the fourth position missing the Olympic Bronze Medal by a whisker.

Ecstatic and exhausted in equal measure on her return from Rio, Dipa Karmakar said she will attempt to continue scripting history wherever she competes.

'I will put every effort to ensure that I keep creating history. My target was to qualify at any cost and I am happy that I have achieved my target', Karmakar told reporters after returning to India to a hero's welcome.

Though Indians applaud Dipa, the gymnast credits her coach for her success. She said, 'It was very difficult but I have got a great mentor because of whom, I am here. Without him nobody would have known my name'. She added, 'To achieve something, you have to take risk. I am thankful to the Sports Authority of India that special arrangements were made at the IG Stadium where I practised and learnt Produnova vault. Otherwise, it would have been impossible'.

What strikes us when we see the stupendous performance by this 22-year-old gymnast is her humility. She constantly brings forward her coach, her father and the Sports Authority as responsible for her success and pays her gratitude to them.

**Think and Say**

When you and your friend won the Tennis Doubles match, your friend spoke only about his own strokes and did not mention you at all. What will you do?

## Remember

- Nothing can be achieved alone. All achievements are the result of many people's contributions.
- India is a great country because its amazing heroes are always humble.
- All sportspeople reach their dreams because they accept learning from their coaches.
- The people of India have always respected their teachers.
- You should never become so proud that you ignore all the people who are supporting you.

## Figure out

**A. Tick the correct answers.**

1. Coach Nandi found it difficult to train six-year-old Dipa because
   a. she was very disobedient and lazy. ☐
   b. she was flat-footed and he had to first train her to bring a curve to her feet. ☐
2. Despite her foot problem, Dipa's father pushed her to take up gymnastics because
   a. he saw in Dipa the qualities of a true sportsperson. ☐
   b. he did not have any concern for her health. ☐
3. From 2007 to 2016, Dipa has been on a winning streak because
   a. she has a lucky charm that makes her win each time. ☐
   b. she works with all her strength and sincerity to do her best. ☐
4. Dipa was given a hero's welcome because
   a. she was part of an Olympics film.
   b. she was the first Indian gymnast to attain fourth place in the final vault at the Olympics and attempt the difficult Produnova vault.
5. Though Dipa is a star performer, she never forgets
   a. to be humble and pay her gratitude to her father, coach and the Sports Authority of India. ☐
   b. to promote her own efforts. ☐

**B. 'I will put every effort to ensure that I keep creating history'. Write the story of another sportsperson for whom this statement is true.**

## Relate

**Tick the best options for the situations given below.**

1. Your brother has spent a lot of effort and time to coach you for the Interschool Badminton Tournament. When you win and people ask for comments. What will you do?
   a. bring your brother forward and give him credit for his coaching ☐
   b. keep praising your own efforts for the win ☐

2. You are very good at creating unique Science models. Your father has ensured that you get good coaching in Science and has bought you equipment you need for your models. When you win a prize at the City Science Exhibition. What will you do?

   a. thank only the judges for giving your model a high score ☐

   b. thank your father and mention his contribution in your achievement ☐

3. Your expertise at cricket is well known, and you have won many awards for your school. But none of it would have been possible without the grounds and coaching your school provided. What will you do?

   a. credit your teachers and the school for every win ☐

   b. happily lap up all the congratulations as your right ☐

4. You have scored the highest marks in the X Boards in the district. The newspaper reporters want to interview you. What will you do?

   a. humbly talk about the efforts of your parents and teachers that contributed to your success ☐

   b. only describe how you didn't sleep for months to study for your success ☐

5. Your teacher has assigned you a project which requires a lot of data collection. What will you do?

   a. Refuse to do it because too much work is involved ☐

   b. Try to do your best and submit the project on time ☐

## Act

## Olympics 2016 Mascot Project

Each Olympics game has a mascot. *Fuwa* or 'good-luck dolls' were the mascots for 2008 Summer Olympics in Beijing. The mascot is a fantasy figure that represents the cultural heritage of the place where the Games are being held.

**Make groups of five students each. Each group finds out and puts together the following information about the mascots of the 2016 Rio Olympics and Paralympics.**

- Who are the mascots?
- What do they symbolize?
- Who designed them?
- If you visit Rio during the Olympics, where would you see them?
- What do you think about the mascots?

## Happiness Box

1. Create an interesting project about the Olympics 2016 Mascot Project using the data collected. The project can also have titbits about the mascots along with pictures. Share your project through a PowerPoint presentation in class.

2. Draw a mascot for your Annual School Sport. Give it a name and explain what it represents.

### Teaching tips

- Emphasize that all of us exist because of the contributions of people like our parents, teachers and many others.
- Reiterate that we must never forget to appreciate their efforts in our lives.
- Remind them that humility is a trait that must be developed in each of us.

# 8. Jakes and the Lady

## Discuss

Look at the pictures. Describe the girl's actions and why she is doing them.

Life Skills

## Read along

*Black Beauty, written in 1877, is an autobiographical memoir of a horse. It not only teaches about loving animals but also how to treat people with kindness, sympathy and respect. The novel was a bestseller.*

I was sold to a corn dealer and baker, whom Jerry knew, and with him he thought I should have good food and fair work. In the first, he was quite right, and if my master had always been on the premises I do not think I should have been overloaded, but there was a foreman who was always hurrying and driving every one, and frequently when I had quite a full load, he would order something else to be taken on. My carter, whose name was Jakes, often said it was more than I ought to take, but the other always overruled him. 'Twas no use going twice when once would do', and he chose to get business forward.

Jakes, like the other carters, always had the check-rein up, which prevented me from drawing easily, and by the time I had been there three or four months, I found the work telling very much on my strength.

One day, I was loaded more than usual, and part of the road was a steep uphill. I used all my strength, but I could not get on and was obliged continually to stop. This did not please my driver, and he laid his whip on badly. 'Get on, you lazy fellow', he said, 'or I'll make you'.

Again, I started the heavy load, and struggled on a few yards; again the whip came down, and again I struggled forward. The pain of that great cart whip was sharp, but my mind was hurt quite as much as my poor sides. To be punished and abused when I was doing my very best was so hard, it took the heart out of me.

A third time he was flogging me cruelly, when a lady stepped quickly up to him, and said in a

in a sweet, earnest voice, 'Oh! Pray do not whip your good horse any more; I am sure heis doing all he can, and the road is very steep; I am sure he is doing his best.'

'If doing his best won't get this load up he must do something more than his best; that's all I know, ma'am,' said Jakes.

'But is it not a heavy load?' she said.

'Yes, yes, too heavy,' he said, 'but that's not my fault; the foreman came just as we were starting, and would have three hundred weight more put on to save him trouble, and I must get on with it as well as I can'.

He was raising the whip again, when the lady said, 'Pray, stop; I think I can help you if you will let me'.

The man laughed.

'You see', she said, 'you do not give him a fair chance; he cannot use all his power with his head held back as it is with that check-rein; if you would take it off I am sure he would do better — do try it', she said persuasively, 'I should be very glad if you would'.

'Well, well,' said Jakes, with a short laugh, 'anything to please a lady, of course. How far would you wish it down, Ma'am?'

'Quite down, give him his head altogether'.

The rein was taken off, and in a moment I put my head down to my very knees. What a comfort it was! Then I tossed it up and down several times to get the aching stiffness out of my neck.

'Poor fellow! That is what you wanted', said she, patting and stroking me with her gentle hand, 'and now if you will speak kindly to him and lead him on I believe he will be able to do better'.

Jakes took the rein. 'Come on, Blackie'. I put down my head, and threw my whole weight against the collar; I spared no strength; the load moved on, and I pulled it steadily up the hill, and then stopped to take breath.

**Think and Say**

You see a woman with a puppy on a leash, barking at a stray dog and the woman beating the stray with a stick. What will you do?

The lady had walked along the footpath, and now came across into the road. She stroked and patted my neck, as I had not been patted for many a long day.

'You see he was quite willing when you gave him the chance; I am sure he is a fine-tempered creature, and I dare say he has known better days. You won't put that rein on again, will you?'

He was just going to hitch it up on the old plan.

'Well, Ma'am, I can't deny that having his head has helped him up the hill, and I'll remember it another time, and thank you, Ma'am; but if he went without a check-rein, I should be the laughing-stock of all the carters; it is the fashion, you see.'

'Is it not better,' she said, 'to lead a good fashion than to follow a bad one? A great many gentlemen do not use check-reins now; our carriage horses have not worn them for fifteen years, and work with much less fatigue than those who have them. 'Besides', she added in a very serious voice, 'we have no right to distress any of God's creatures without a very good reason. We call them dumb animals, and so they are, for they cannot tell us how they feel, but they do not suffer less because they have no words. But I must not detain you now; I thank you for trying my plan with your good horse, and I am sure you will find it far better than the whip. Good-day'.

And with another soft pat on my neck she stepped lightly across the path, and I saw her no more.

*—Adapted from Black Beauty by Anna Sewell*

## Safe and Unsafe Touches and Looks

**Personal Safety**

Touches and looks are related to our body safety. Most, but not all, touches and looks are safe. We should learn to understand the difference between various types of touches, looks and feelings. Touches can be loving, caring, accidental or hurtful. If you encounter someone whose touch or looks make you feel scared or unsafe, do the following safety drill: Scream or Say No, Run, Tell, Keep telling till someone believes you.

## Remember

- Show that you value the lives of animals by being patient with them, giving them plenty of water and food, taking them out for walks and regular health checks.
- Allow pet animals to live with you in your homes, play with them and spend time with them.
- Sometimes tiny animals wander into your house. Show them the way out without using violence.
- Never ever hit animals.
- Avoid games that show cruelty to animals.

## Figure out

**A. Tick the correct answers.**

1. Why did the horse find the work tiring?
   a. The horse was lazy and didn't like hard work. ☐
   b. The horse cart was always overloaded and restricted by the check-rein that made pulling the cart more tiring. ☐
2. What hurt the horse's mind and took the heart out of him?
   a. The horse was doing his best to pull the load and yet the carter was constantly whipping him. ☐
   b. The horse missed all his friends with whom he wanted to play. ☐
3. How did the lady stop his torture by the carter?
   a. The lady bought the horse from the carter. ☐
   b. The lady pleaded with the carter not to whip the horse and to take off the check-rein. ☐
4. Why did the horse put all his strength to pull the load up the hill?
   a. He realized that if he was lazy, he will be whipped. ☐
   b. The lady's kind words and taking off the check-rein motivated the horse to use all his strength. ☐
5. What made the carter different from the lady?
   a. The carter was a man with a job to be done unlike the lady. ☐
   b. The carter was selfish and did not care about the horse's pain while the lady was kind and wanted to help the horse. ☐

B. 'Is it not better,' she said, 'to lead a good fashion than to follow a bad one? Do you agree with her?

## Relate

**Tick the best options for the situations given below.**

1. You find that your neighbour keeps his pet dog in a small cage in the yard because he is in office all day. What will you do?
   a. request your neighbour to uncage the dog and offer to look after it during the day ☐
   b. ignore what you have seen ☐
2. You have had a bad day but when you enter your home, your pet puppy jumps up to greet you. What will you do
   a. kick it away because its licks irritate you ☐
   b. hug your puppy because its love wipes out your unhappiness ☐
3. Early each morning the birds on the tree outside your bedroom start singing and you cannot sleep late even when you want to. What will you do?
   a. enjoy the birdsongs at dawn and count it as a blessing from nature ☐
   b. ask to get the tree cut so that the birds cannot sing on its branches and disturb your sleep ☐
4. Your friend has been gifted with a small aquarium. She loves fishes. So she packs the tank with lots of fish. What will you do?
   a. explain how all the fish are suffering without space and convince her to let them float away in a stream ☐
   b. gift her some more fish so that you become her best friend ☐

## Act

## Adopt a Park

**Make groups of five students each in your class. Each group must adopt a park for one week.**

Carry out activities like picking up garbage like empty bottles and plastic wrappers that disturb small creatures like worms, plant seedlings, nurture flowers for bees and butterflies, and ensure that the walking paths are clean so that dogs and pets can be exercised.

Make a weekly activity chart that records your actions, and at the end of the week, put it up in class.

## Happiness Box

1. **During your 'Adopt a Park' week, make posters to create awareness about active compassion towards animals. You can take ideas from the one given here.**

2. **Divide your class into three groups.**

   Each group must gather information about any one of the three types of dogs given below. Then each group gives a PowerPoint presentation about it to the class.

   - Guide dog for the visually impaired.
   - Farm dog for herding sheep.
   - Police dog to help catch criminals.

**Teaching tips**

- Reiterate that animals have feelings just like we do. So we must ensure that we don't hurt their feelings.
- Taking care of pets is a regular activity and is a duty we have towards them.
- Remind students that animals also take care of us in many ways

# 9. The Fridge that Feeds

## Discuss

**Look at the pictures and discuss in the class.**

Never stop doing little things for others. Their smiles are our biggest gift .

## Read along

**News Times**

**A PUBLIC FRIDGE**

SUTAPA DAS
MAY 2, 2016

A 'heroic' fridge has taken the onus of bringing smiles to the faces of the destitute and has become a source of happiness for hundreds in Kochi. The poor and homeless in Kochi's Kaloor area don't have to worry any more about scavenging for food. There is a ready supply of fresh, healthy food available daily, all thanks to a restaurant's generous owner.

Called '*Nanma Maram*' or the 'Tree of Goodness', this refrigerator has been installed outside a restaurant, *Pappadavada*, where anyone can drop off left over food— and that food, in turn, can be picked up by the hungry and the homeless. The fridge works 24/7. It's located at Kaloor-Kathrikadavu road in Kochi.

'We bear the cost of the fridge and the electricity, and keep it open for 24 hours a day', says the owner of Pappadavada.

Minu Pauline, who started Pappadavada in 2013 after quitting the banking industry, aims to reduce food wastage in cities. And through her efforts, she keeps the homeless fed and healthy. She says, 'Food is a precious gift from nature and people should not waste it. The sole purpose of this initiative is to give food that is in excess for some to those who are less fortunate to buy it.'

The idea struck Minu when she heard about the 'coffee on the wall' concept common in many countries and it inspired her to do her bit to feed the poor. This 'public fridge' functions around the clock, and the response from the public, so far, has been amazing. While many buy food specially to contribute to the fridge, Minu encourages locals to bring the leftover food from their own homes which would otherwise be wasted. All they need to make sure is that the food is fresh and packed properly.

Pappadavadam not only

takes up the expense and upkeep of the fridge, but also ensures that 50 individually wrapped parcels of food are in it every single day. The fridge has a marker in it, so every food donor can fill out the date of packing to ensure the food is consumed before becoming stale.

And how would someone avoid the whole pilfering angle of it all? I have just put my faith in the goodness of people,' Minu told *NewsTimes* during an interview.

One person's small act of kindness can inspire many others to make a difference as well. We, at *NewsTimes*, also started exploring how we could help the under privileged. Eventually, it was decided that our staff would contribute to the public fridge by sponsoring a whole month of food packages that are prepared by Pappadavadam. The contributors felt satisfied to know that somewhere for someone they have made a difference.

**Think and Say**

Your teacher is dictating the notes for a difficult Math topic, but your friend is absent. What will you do?

## Remember

- Caring is a two-way route. When you bring happiness to others, you make yourself happy.
- You must open your heart to feel the pain of others.
- Caring goes beyond your own family and friends. It includes needy people animals and birds, our earth and the environment.
- Caring people are usually gentle people. This gentleness is not weakness. It is their strength.
- Caring must be shown through your speech and your actions.

## Figure out

**A. Tick the correct answers.**

1. Why is the public fridge called 'heroic'?
   a. It has brought happiness to hundreds of poor and homeless people. ☐
   b. It is made by a company called Heroic. ☐
2. How does the public fridge work?
   a. It uses electricity through a cable connected to the restaurant. ☐
   b. Anytime, people can drop off food packages at the fridge which are picked up by the hungry and homeless. ☐

3. What was Minu Pauline's aim in installing this fridge?

   a. She wanted to ensure that excess food in homes is not wasted, but goes to the poor people who need food.

   b. She wanted to become a popular heroine of the people of Kochi.

4. Have the people liked Minu's idea?

   a. In fact, nobody brings any excess food to keep in the fridge.

   b. Not only do people bring their leftover food, they even buy food to keep in the fridge every day.

5. How did it inspire the *NewsTimes* staff?

   a. They decided to contribute to a month's expense of the fifty food packages that Pappadavadam keeps daily in the fridge.

   b. They clicked a lot of photographs of the fridge and printed it in their magazine.

**B. Write a story or an incident that illustrates, 'If you really care, you will always find time to show it'.**

## Relate

**Tick the best options for the situations given below.**

1. You buy a bottle of cold drink. Suddenly, you see a young street child watching you from the roadside. What will you do?

   a. ignore him as you cannot buy drinks for every street child

   b. hand over the cold drink to the child as he needs it more than you

2. Your mother gets up very early to help you go to school. She also sleeps late because she has to complete all the housework at night. What will you do?

   a. watch TV for lesser time and help your mother with the housework?

   b. not bother as all mothers have this kind of schedule

3. You have baked a cake for the first time with your father's help. You get to know that it is your house help's daughter's birthday. What will you do?

   a. give your house help one small piece for the child because your family wants to eat the cake

   b. give the whole cake to your househelp for her daughter as you can bake another cake for the family the next day

4. You see your elderly neighbour slowly cleaning her garden though she is unable to bend and pick up the rubbish. What will you do
   a. turn away as you have enough work to do at home? ☐
   b. quickly go over to help her finish cleaning her garden in lesser time ☐

## Act

### Enact Out

1. Make pairs.
2. Each pair has to collaborate to act out this statement, 'We are not machines. We are human beings'.
3. While acting you must use only actions, gestures and facial expressions, but silently. You cannot speak any words.

## Happiness Box

### Make a Collage

1. Take photographs of a family member while he or she is doing caring things for the family and make a collage of the photos with suitable captions. Share your collage in class.
2. Write a newspaper report about an incident in which a young girl tries to rescue her sister from a fire at home not caring about her own safety.

**Teaching tips**

- Reiterate that caring for others is always without expectations.
- Remind students that when they care for others, others will also care for them.
- Make them understand that genuine feelings of caring come from the heart.

# 10. Slotting Your Time

## Discuss

**Look and discuss in class.**

Is that your day?

**Effective Time management**

| MY DAY | |
|---|---|
| 7:00–10:00 am | SLEEP |
| 10:00–10:30 am | EAT |
| 10:30–12:00 pm | SLEEP |
| 12:00–12:30 pm | EAT AND DRINK |
| 12:30–1:00 pm | SAND BOX |
| 1:00–4:00 pm | SLEEP |
| 4:00–4:30 pm | CHEW BONE |
| 4:30–8:00 pm | SLEEP |
| 8:00 pm | DAY OVER |

## Read along

A teacher stood before his class. On a table in front of him was a large empty glass jar and a big cardboard box. Without a word, from the box, he started taking out large rocks and putting them in the jar. He filled it to the top until not one rock could go in.

Then he asked the students in his class, 'Is the jar full?'

They said, 'Yes Sir. It is full'.

Then the teacher took small pebbles from the box and started putting them in the jar. He shook the jar and the pebbles rolled into the spaces between the rocks.

When there was no more space for pebbles to fill, he asked the class, 'Is the jar full?'

The class answered in unison, 'Oh yes, Sir'.

Then the teacher put his hand back into the box. His fist came out filled with sand. He started pouring the sand into the jar. It slipped and slid into the tiny spaces between the rocks and the pebbles. The teacher kept doing it till the jar was filled to the brim with sand.

Then he said, 'This jar is your life'. He went on, 'The rocks are the most important things in your life, such as your family, friends and your health. Without them, you will be nearly destroyed. The pebbles are the next important things, such as your house, your bicycle, your TV and other things that make you happy. The sand is everything else. You know, the 'small stuff, such as an ice cream, a video game, a match you want to win'.

The class stared at the jar trying to understand what the teacher was saying.

He continued, 'If you put the pebbles or the sand into the jar first there will be no place for the rocks. Similarly, if you spend all your time and energy on less important or the small things of life, you will have no time for the truly important things of life.
So pay attention to things that are really important and spend time on them.

**Think and Say**

To prepare for the Interschool Tennis Championships, your coach wants you to practise for two hours daily but your friend is asking you to go with him to a film show. What will you do?

Then he put up a poster in the class. On it was a list.

**Some Truly Important Things**

- Spend time with your family.
- Spend time with your friends.
- Spend time with your grandparents.
- Take time to exercise.
- Take time to improve yourself.
- Find time to think how to become a better person.
- Spend time on preventing rather than on solving problems
- Take care of the rocks first - the things that really matter.
- Set your priorities. The rest is just pebbles and sand.
- Believe in yourself, know what you want and make it happen!

## Remember

- List all the things that you absolutely have to do.
- Create a timetable for your day to slot all your activities.
- Be flexible but realistic when making the slots.
- You must take time out to research and plan to make a good timetable.
- Avoid delaying work and things that distract you from it.
- Try doing physical exercise like walking in between study slots to clear your mind.

## Figure out

**A. Tick the correct answers.**

1. According to the teacher, if the jar was life, what did he first fill in it?
   a. Important things like family, friends and health ☐
   b. Big rocks ☐
2. Next what did the teacher fill in the jar of life?
   a. The teacher filled pebbles in the jar. ☐
   b. The teacher filled things that make us happy, such as house, bicycle into the jar representing life. ☐

3. What was the next thing that should be filled in life
   a. All the small things of life that matter only for a moment
   b. Handful of sand
4. How does the teacher advise us to deal with life?
   a. We should first take care of all things of comfort and luxury that we need.
   b. We should spend our time and energy on the most important things and the small things will take care of themselves.
5. What was the final statement on the poster that the teacher put up?
   a. We should enjoy all the good things that life offers us.
   b. We should set priorities in life, believe in ourselves and make our dreams happen by our efforts.
6. Which of these was on the teacher's list?
   a. Spend time with your family.
   b. Spend time with your pets.

**B. Write a story or incident to illustrate this statement, 'Take care of the big rocks first, the rest are just sand and pebbles.'**

## Relate

**Tick the best options for the situations given below.**

1. You have an important Math assignment to complete in the evening exactly when a winning cricket match is being aired too. What will you do?
   a. do your assignment in front of the TV watching the match even though it will be a distraction
   b. complete your assignment and then watch the final stages of the match
2. Your mother has saved money to buy you and your sister winter jackets but you want a video game. What will you do?
   a. throw a tantrum and insist your mother buy you the game with the saved money
   b. sacrifice your desire because the jackets will help you to be in good health

3. Your family goes out together in an old, noisy car and your friends make fun of it. What will you do?

   a. accept the jokes your friends make about your car with a smile ☐

   b. insist your father buy a new car even if he has to take a loan and worry about returning it ☐

4. Your mother is very sick but you have already planned to go on a school picnic. What will you do?

   a. go on the picnic because your enjoyment with your friends is more important to you? ☐

   b. cancel the picnic plan and spend the whole day with your mother? ☐

## Act

## Timetable Survey

**1. Conduct a survey on the topic, How do I use my time? Find out your scores on how well you use study time. Work in pairs. Ask your partner questions to fill this survey sheet.**

**How Do I Use My Time?**

Think back over the last 24 hours and calculate how much time you have spent on the following activities.

I spent

1. ________________ minutes on sleeping.
2. ________________ minutes with my family.
3. ________________ minutes eating.
4. ________________ minutes on TV or video games.
5. ________________ minutes talking to my friends.
6. ________________ minutes on other activities.

2. Find out how your partner studies. Ask questions on how your partner studies and allocate marks. If the answer to the questions below is 'always', give 3 points. If the answer is 'some times', give 2 points. If the answer is 'probably not', give 1 point.

1. I have a regular time for studying each day. _______________
2. I write my assignments down and check the list regularly. _______________
3. I always have the materials I need when I start to study. _______________
4. I rarely distract myself by wandering away from the task when studying. _______________
5. I do assignments in chunks to avoid last minute work. _______________

## Happiness Box

### Time Management Card

1. Based on the data collected during the survey for 'How do I use my time?', make this Time Management Card for your partner. You must discuss the data collected during the survey with your partner. Then fill answers to the questions and share your Time Management Card in class.

| Name of student ________________________ | |
|---|---|
| **Data and questions** | **Answers filled by the student** |
| What are the things you do sometimes and not every day? | |
| What are the things you need to do regularly every day? | |
| What are the really important things in your life that need more time? | |
| What is that one thing you spend a lot of time on that can be done away with? | |

2. This word search has 10 words related to time. Choose a time keeper. When the time keeper says, 'Start', you should start searching for the words. The time keeper will say 'Stop' after 10 minutes, and you should stop searching. The students who have found all ten or most words are the winners.

| | | | | | | | | | | | |
|---|---|---|---|---|---|---|---|---|---|---|---|
| K | L | O | P | H | G | B | F | G | T | Y | G |
| M | G | S | L | O | T | C | J | U | Y | H | G |
| I | H | U | J | V | N | A | N | A | L | O | G |
| L | P | N | O | E | C | L | O | C | K | Y | P |
| L | E | R | E | R | W | E | O | V | G | H | U |
| E | I | I | U | T | Y | N | N | B | C | V | N |
| N | O | S | U | I | Y | D | Q | Z | X | C | C |
| N | F | E | T | M | H | A | B | G | F | R | T |
| I | U | I | O | E | O | R | B | G | G | B | U |
| U | O | P | R | E | W | A | Q | Z | C | F | A |
| M | F | O | R | T | N | I | G | H | T | Y | L |
| A | K | J | U | O | P | G | F | R | R | T | H |

**Teaching tips**

- Reiterate that managing time is a skill that is necessary when taking exams.
- Making a timetable helps one to complete all the scheduled work comfortably leaving sufficient time for rest and relaxation.
- Remind students to avoid all distracters that waste time.

# 11. If

## Discuss

**Read and discuss in class.**

'What light is to eyes; what air is to lungs; what love is to heart liberty is to the soul of man.'

Integrity is doing the right thing when nobody is watching.

## Read along

If you can keep your head when all about you
Are losing theirs and blaming it on you,
If you can trust yourself when all men doubt you,
But make allowance for their doubting too;
If you can wait and not be tired by waiting,
Or being lied about, don't deal in lies,
Or being hated, don't give way to hating,
And yet don't look too good, nor talk too wise:

If you can dream—and not make dreams your master;
If you can think—and not make thoughts your aim;
If you can meet with Triumph and Disaster
And treat those two imposters just the same;
If you can bear to hear the truth you've spoken . . .
Or watch the things you gave your life to, broken,
And stoop and build 'em up with worn-out tools:

If you can talk with crowds and keep your virtue,
Or walk with Kings—nor lose the common touch,
If neither foes nor loving friends can hurt you,
If all men count with you, but none too much;
If you can fill the unforgiving minute
With sixty seconds' worth of distance run,
Yours is the Earth and everything that's in it,
And—which is more—you'll be a Man, my son!

*—Rudyard Kipling*

### Think and Say

You want to give a rose to your teacher on Teachers' Day. There is none in your garden but one blooming in your neighbour's garden. Nobody is around. What will you do?

## Figure out

**A. Tick the correct answers.**

1. If you know in your heart that you are faultless,
   a. you will retain your self-confidence even when everyone is blaming you. ☐
   b. still you are unsure whether any one of your actions was wrong. ☐
2. When people lie to you or hate you, you must
   a. return the same lies and hatred to them. ☐
   b. stop yourself from lying to or hating them. ☐
3. You will always have a stable mind, if you
   a. do not glorify your victories or be depressed at your failures. ☐
   b. promote your victories and hide your failures. ☐
4. Integrity is respected when
   a. you respect the important people and ignore the lesser important ones. ☐
   b. you respect everyone equally and do not give special favours to anyone. ☐
5. You will be a confident, upright person, if you
   a. use every minute of your life to work hard and with honesty for the benefit of others. ☐
   b. use every minute of your life to work for your own selfish needs. ☐

**B. 'Live so that when your children think of fairness, caring and integrity, they think of you,' said H. Jackson Brown, Jr., an inspirational author. Write about a person whose life reminds you of these qualities.**

## Relate

**Tick the best options for the situations given below.**

1. You have forgotten to bring your snack for the recess and are feeling very hungry. After recess, you pass the school snack store and the owner is not there. You have no money. What will you do?
   a. pick up a packet of wafers without paying for it ☐
   b. request the owner to give you a packet of snacks and promise to pay him the next day ☐

2. Your sibling and you quarrel. Both of you are at fault but your mother scolds you. You find your sibling alone at home. What will you do?

   a. try to resolve your argument peacefully ☐

   b. fight with him or her to avenge being scolded ☐

3. As the class monitor, you penalize students for coming late to class. Your best friend comes in late. What will you do?

   a. ignore that he or she has broken the rule because of your friendship ☐

   b. penalize your friend because your integrity says everyone must be treated equally ☐

4. Being very busy as the class monitor, you are unable to complete your assignment. What will you do?

   a. accept the penalty that your teacher gives to all students who have not submitted their assignment ☐

   b. ask your teacher to excuse you because you are the class monitor ☐

## Act

## Honesty is the Best Policy

**Divide the class into two teams. Each team role plays one of the following situations.**

**Situation 1:** Shopkeeper sells a broken, glued-together phone to a customer. The next day, the customer comes back angry at being cheated. He tells his story to everyone in the market. They make the shopkeeper close his store.

**Situation 2:** Customer chooses a phone from the store's shelf. The shopkeeper shows him that it is a broken phone and offers him another one. The customer is very happy and tells other people in the market. Everyone comes to the store to buy phones.

### Happiness Box

1. **Truthfulness, integrity and straightforwardness are all attributes of honesty. Lying, stealing and cheating are dishonest practices. Read stories on honesty written in different books and even in varied languages from the Internet or listen to such stories from adults in the family.**

   Now make a storyboard of any one story on honesty and display it on the bulletin board. You can even make a PowerPoint presentation on honesty.

2. **Put a musical tune to this poem and sing it to your class.**

**The Boy Who Never Told a Lie**

Once there was a little boy.
With curly hair and pleasant eye—
A boy who always told the truth,
And never, never told a lie

And when he trotted off to school,
The children all about would cry,
'There goes the curly-headed boy—
The boy who never tells a lie'.

And everybody loved him so,
Because he always told the truth.
That every day, as he grew up,
'Twas said, 'There goes the honest youth'

And when the people that stood near
Would turn to ask the reason why,
The answer would be always this:
'Because he never tells a lie'

—*Anonymous*

**Teaching tips**

- Reiterate that integrity and honesty should be part of character. They are not for promoting one's popularity.
- Remind students that honest people are considered dependable.
- Stress that one must tell the truth, however difficult it may be.

# 12. Victory or Defeat

## Discuss

**Look at the picture. What do you think is about to happen? Discuss in class.**

## Read along

Emperor Ashoka was one of the most powerful kings of the Indian subcontinent. A ruler of the Mauryan Empire, Ashoka ruled over the country from 273 BC to 232 BC. His kingdom covered most of India and South Asia.

Eight years after ascending the throne of Magadha, Emperor Ashoka attacked Kalinga to the east of his kingdom. Being proud, freedom-loving people, the Kalinga army displayed extraordinary courage or foolhardiness and put up a brave fight against the mighty Maghadan. Ashoka was merciless in wreaking vengeance against his weaker adversary. Sheer bloodbath followed.

As the legend goes, after the battle of Kalinga, Ashoka went to the devastated battlefield to inspect the valiant deeds of his brave soldiers. However, he did not see any sign of victory. All he saw were heaps of rotting and burning corpses and half-dead bodies of injured people wailing in pain. Severe sorrow and remorse gripped his conscience. The legend describes his state of mind in this monologue.

*'What have I done? If this is a victory, what's a defeat then? Is this a victory or a defeat? Is this justice or injustice? Is it gallantry or a rout? Is it valour to kill innocent children and women? Do I do it to widen the empire and for prosperity or to destroy other's kingdom and splendour? One has lost her husband, someone else a father, someone a child, someone an unborn infant . . . What's this debris of the corpses? Are these marks of victory or defeat? Are these vultures, crows, eagles, the messengers of death or evil?'*

**On Ashoka's Rock Edict 13, we can read these words:**

Beloved-of-the-Gods, King Piyadasi, conquered the Kalingas eight years after his coronation. One hundred and fifty thousand were deported, one hundred thousand were killed and many more died (from other causes). After the Kalingas had been conquered, Beloved-of-the-gods came to feel a strong inclination towards the Dhamma, a love forthe Dhamma and for instruction in Dhamma. Now Beloved of-the-Gods feels deep remorse for having conquered the Kalingas.

The horror of this ghastly war was a life-altering experience for the mighty Magadha ruler.

Emperor Ashoka turned into a philosopher-king, who ruled by being an example of rectitude and selfless service to his people. He embraced the basic principles of Buddhism. Ashoka's Dharma was based on the principles of non-violence, tolerance,

piety, mercy, kindness, generosity, truthfulness, forgiveness, purity, gentleness, goodness and peaceful coexistence of all religions. He spread Buddha's philosophy across the land. He even sent emissaries to foreign countries to spread the message of Dhamma. He discouraged people from killing animals for food and sacrifices, and even burning the kernels of grains. He declared that good behaviour earns its fruits, here on earth and hereafter, far better than by performing *Yajnas*. He had his edicts carved in stone all over his kingdom. In these edicts, he spoke plainly in the people's own language. He made sure that all people across his vast empire knew exactly what he thought and what he expected of them.

Rock edicts of King Ashoka

Emperor Asoka built thousands of stupas and *viharas*. One of his stupas, the Great Sanchi Stupa, has been declared a World Heritage Site by UNECSO. The capital of Ashoka Pillar at Sarnath that has four lions facing the four directions has been adopted as the national emblem of the Republic of India. The Ashoka Chakra from the base of the Lion Capital is displayed on the Indian Tricolour.

Sanchi Stupa

**Think and Say**

Your friend loves hitting birds with a catapult while you hate seeing birds suffer. What will you do?

## Remember

- All issues can be solved peacefully.
- Fighting only brings hurt and hatred. It makes others fight back.
- Talking calmly and softly can cool down angry people.
- Always keep your own anger in control.
- People who can do things peacefully are wanted as peacemakers everywhere.

## Figure out

**A. Tick the correct answers.**

1. Why did King Ashoka attack Kalinga?
   a. King Ashoka's kingdom was over populated and he needed more land. ☐
   b. King Ashoka wanted to defeat the proud Kalingans. ☐
2. Why did Ashoka feel sorrow and remorse after the battle?
   a. He blamed himself for the death and destruction that was the result of his war with Kalinga. ☐
   b. He had been defeated by the brave Kalingans. ☐
3. How did this sad experience change King Ashoka's approach to life?
   a. King Ashoka became so depressed that he was ill. ☐
   b. King Ashoka became a philosopher-king. He was righteous and gave selfless service to his people. ☐
4. What did his edicts say?
   a. His edicts declared all his victories in wars. ☐
   b. His edicts said that only good behaviour earns its fruits in this life and later, not animal sacrifices. They discouraged people from killing animals. ☐
5. Why is King Ashoka important in Modern India?
   a. Modern Indians even today follow him by declaring war on other countries. ☐
   b. King Ashoka's philosophy of peaceful coexistence is followed by Modern India. ☐
6. Which of these is a UNESCO World Heritage Site?
   a. Rock edicts of Ashoka ☐
   b. Sanchi Stupa ☐

**B. 'War is the only way that one country can dominate another.' Do you agree with the statement?**

## Relate

**Tick the best options for the situations given below.**

1. A naughty classmate is always teasing and troubling others. Everyone is angry with him and want to teach him a lesson. What will you do?
    a. sit down with him and explain to him how his behaviour is making him friendless ☐
    b. gang up against him and fight with him to make him change ☐
2. Your classmate scores as much marks as you at Math by copying from your answer sheet. What will you do?
    a. confront him or her at recess and even threaten to complain to the teacher ☐
    b. offer to help for the next test and convince him or her to work hard ☐
3. You have unintentionally pushed a teammate during a football match. The person wants to fight with you for it. What will you do?
    a. aggressively challenge him to a fight ☐
    b. apologise to the person and explain that you did not mean to push him ☐
4. The news on TV says that if the talks between two countries break down, they could go to war. Your sister is excited that she will be able to watch scenes from a real war on TV. What will you do?
    a. describe to her all the death, destruction and sorrow that war creates ☐
    b happily agree and wait eagerly for the talks to break down ☐

## Act

# Open-mic Day

1. Write topics related to peace on notes. Roll them up and put all notes in a bowl.
2. Students will pick up a note and speak for 1 minute on the topic without pausing.
3. Some topics could be:
    - Peace is the answer to all problems.
    - Can war solve anything?
    - To have peace, do we prepare for war?

## Happiness Box

# World Peace Day

1. **21st September is the World Peace Day.**

   Wear a 'Peace Badge' and smile at everyone you see on that day, even if you may not know them.

   **Make a Peace Badge**

   1. Draw this picture on a stiff paper, 2×2 inches.
   2. Stick the picture on a piece of felt that has been cut the same size.
   3. Pin the badge to your shirt.

2. **Dramatize the story of King Ashoka's regret after the Kalinga War changing him into a philosopher-king. Then gather your friends and enact the play.**

### Teaching tips

- Remind students that peacemakers are more popular than fighters.
- Reiterate that all problems are solved better peacefully.
- Stress how anger destroys while peace builds everything.

# Goal 5: Gender Equality

- On an average, women do three times as much unpaid care and domestic work as men.
- Less than one out of three senior and middle management positions are held by women.
- 49 countries have no law specifically protecting women from domestic violence.

The Indian Constitution has enacted several laws to promote gender equality and women empowerment
Read. Imbibe. Practice.
Take A Stand!

International Women's Day (IWD) is celebrated on the 8 March every year around the world.

## Spread Awareness!

- End all forms of discrimination against girls and women.
- Enhance use of technology, especially communications technology, to promote the empowerment of women.

**National Commission for Women Act, 1990**

## Equality at Home

- Share responsibility equally between men and women, within the household.
- Stop harmful traditional practices like child marriage.
- Provide equal education for both boys and girls to make them independent.

**Right of Children to Free and Compulsory Education Act, 2009**

## Equality at Workplace

- Ensure women's full and effective participation as well as equal opportunities for leadership at all levels of decision making - in political, economic and public life.

**Equal Remuneration Act, 1976**

# Project III : Gymnastics

**Dipa Karmakar has become celebrity the world over for her excellent performance of the Produnova vault in the field of gymnastics. Find out everything you can about the Produnova vault and write a project report on it.**

You can use the following points in your report.

- What is the Produnova vault?
- History of the vault
- Risks of attempting the vault
- Effort put in by Dipa Karmakar to master the vault

# Project IV : Save Animals

**Your birdbath has made birds happy but did you know that many animals are ill-treated and neglected right in your city. To care for these animals, organizations have opened animal rescue shelters. Find out more about two such shelters and write a report on them. You may use these points in your report.**

- How does the animal rescue shelter work?
- Which animals can one generally find in these shelters?
- Describe the shelters. (If you can visit one, it would be best)
- Find out how many other such shelters are there in your city or town.

..................................................................................................................

..................................................................................................................

..................................................................................................................

..................................................................................................................

..................................................................................................................

..................................................................................................................

..................................................................................................................

..................................................................................................................

..................................................................................................................

..................................................................................................................

..................................................................................................................

..................................................................................................................

..................................................................................................................

..................................................................................................................

..................................................................................................................

..................................................................................................................

..................................................................................................................

..................................................................................................................